Will Our Children
Have Faith?

WILL

OUR CHILDREN

HAVE FAITH?

John H. Westerhoff III

Harper & Row, Publishers, San Francisco
Cambridge, Hagerstown, New York, Philadelphia
London, Mexico City, São Paulo, Singapore, Sydney

Library of Congress Catalog Card Number: 76-21258
ISBN: 0-86683-952-6 (previously ISBN: 0-8164-2435-7)

Printed in the United States of America
5   4   3   2

DEDICATED TO

my wife Barnie

and our children Jill, Jack, and Beth;

my faculty and student colleagues

at Duke University Divinity School;

my friends, supporters, and critics,

lay and clergy, throughout the Church.

CONTENTS

Preface   *ix*

CHAPTER ONE
The Shaking of the Foundations   *1*

CHAPTER TWO
Beginning and Ending with Faith   *26*

CHAPTER THREE
In Search of Community   *51*

CHAPTER FOUR
Life Together   *79*

CHAPTER FIVE
Hope for the Future   *104*

Preface

Will Our Children Have Faith? marks an end and a beginning in my pilgrimage, a journey which began in 1970 when I penned my first tract, *Values For Tomorrow's Children* (Pilgrim 1970) as a challenge to dream of an alternative future for the church's educational mission and ministry.

As founder-editor of *Colloquy* magazine, I found that there were others who shared my concerns and had important contributions to make. *A Colloquy On Christian Education* (Pilgrim 1972) provided an opportunity to collect and share their thoughts.

Then as my mind began to frame a response to my earlier challenge, I discovered the importance of religious socialization. Gwen Kennedy Neville joined me in a dialogue, *Generation To Generation* (Pilgrim 1974), which helped to frame the foundational nature of the church's educational problem.

Now I am ready to take a stand: to propose an alternative framework for evaluating, planning, and engaging in religious education. However, like my first book, this is also a tract. Its purpose is to stimulate reflection, conversation, and perhaps debate. In the last two decades there has been too little passionate discussion about the shape of education in the church.

Will Our Children Have Faith?

Today while some people are paralyzed by discouragement, others are all too enthusiastically latching onto every new suggestion or idea. But too few are engaged in serious argument about the nature and purpose of religious education. Not since the clash between proponents of progressive education and their neo-orthodox critics in the 30s has anyone been able to raise more than a whisper on crucial foundational issues. Without such discussion we are not likely to find the way out of our current morass. This book, then, is an invitation to engage ourselves in renewed conversations about the future of religious education, to debate foundational issues, and to rethink the Church's educational mission and ministry.

My definition of a professor is one who professes what she or he believes at the moment in order to stimulate people to think for themselves. But that explains only part of my purpose in writing this book; the other has to do with convictions: I *believe* what I have written, and I hope that my thesis will be found acceptable and valuable. More important, however, is the necessary struggle and continuing quest to frame an alternative future for religious education.

That is what I meant when I said this book marked an end and a beginning. Now the hard, slow process of systematic critique, the engagement in new research, the expansion of investigations in foundational issues, and the development and testing of concrete programs begins. Your help is needed. I've spoken a first word, the last should not be spoken too soon.

Hundreds of letters have come to me as a result of my earlier books. Each one is valuable, both the positive and the negative, because each has helped me proceed to this turning point in my work. I'm grateful. Now your comments and criticisms are needed once again. All of us—lay persons and clergy, professionals and nonprofessionals—are in this together. *Will Our Children Have Faith?* may seem like a dramatic title, but from my point of view it clearly and forcefully states the issue we face. We are engaged in very serious business. In this "tract for the times," I've attempted to surface afresh the issue of faith and suggest implications for our educational ministry. The stakes are high and the ultimate solution belongs to all of us.

Of course I have not done all this work alone. My friends have influenced my views. While they should not be held responsible for my errors, I do want to acknowledge appreciation. The important and relevant work of James Fowler both inspired and informed me. McMurry Richey, my colleague in religious education and H. Shelton Smith, my predecessor at Duke, provided me with the necessary encouragement to take on this awesome task.

My wife and children especially deserve mention, for without their support and sacrifices I never would have completed this work. Lesta Gotsch, my faithful secretary, struggled with my poor penmanship and helped me meet the pressure of deadlines. Further, I want to express appreciation to Ted McConnell who, as my editor, once again helped me immeasurably.

There are thousands of lay persons and clergy throughout the country who have been with me on one occasion or another. While they will have to go unnamed, I want them to know that this book would not have been written without their aid. Then there are also the students in my research seminar at Duke who helped me to test my thoughts: Lee Bryant, Milton Carothers, Heather Elkins, Pamela Ford, Gary Greene, Deborah Hemenway, Boyd Holiday,

Will Our Children Have Faith?

Kenneth Kelly, Timothy Kimbey, Susan Levis, Steven Rainey, Susan Thistlethwaite, Rachel Tucker, Margaret Turbyfill.

One last important note of gratitude. This book was first presented as the Robert F. Jones Lectures at Austin Presbyterian Theological Seminary, Austin, Texas. I want to thank the First Presbyterian Church, Forth Worth, Texas, who endowed that lectureship; Dr. Robert F. Jones and his wife Annetta W. Jones, after whom they were named; and the Austin seminary faculty, students, and alumni whose affirmations and encouragement gave me the courage to complete the book. In one important sense this book finalizes one period in my life; it also ushers in a new one. I offer you my present thoughts with humility and not just a little fear and trembling. May they not go unjudged by God's redeeming spirit.

John H. Westerhoff III

Lent 1976
Duke University Divinity School
Durham, North Carolina

Will Our Children
Have Faith?

CHAPTER ONE

The Shaking of the
Foundations

The immediate future of liberal Protestant education is un-
certain. Despite its appearance of modernity and relentless
relevance, mainstream Protestantism is rooted in the ethos of
the last century. [The issue that faces us is] do we have the
courage to acknowledge the shaking of the foundations?
Robert W. Lynn

IT IS A TRUISM that Christian faith and education are
inevitable companions. Wherever living faith exists, there is
a community endeavoring to know, understand, live, and
witness to that faith. Still, an accurate description of education in the church today is difficult. Here and there exemplary educational ministries flourish, but in many more
places anxiety, confusion, frustration, despair, and even
failure exist. While generalizations may be difficult, few
would defend the contemporary health and vitality of
Christian education within mainline Protestant Churches.
Since 1957 when *Life* magazine dubbed the Sunday school
the most wasted hour of the week, increasing numbers of

church persons have admitted that their educational ministries are less than adequate for the day. The church school, despite numerous bold innovations and even a few modern success stories, is plagued with disease. There may be disagreement over the severity of the illness and the prognosis of recovery, but there is no debate as to whether or not all is well. Differing diagnoses, however, do exist. For example, it appears that many church educators are sure that we are dealing with a surface infection, while I am convinced that we face a very serious disease.

This conviction is not entirely new. *Colloquy* was born in 1968 and for eight years, as founder and editor, I advocated the need for radical change in church education. In 1970, just before the walls of mainline Protestant church education began to show its cracks, I published a series of works which boldly suggested that an alternative for church education was needed. I have now concluded that it is not enough simply to conceive of alternative programs for church education; fundamental issues once clearly resolved need to be explored afresh. No longer can we assume that the educational understandings that have informed us, or the theological foundations that have undergirded our efforts, are adequate for the future. A continuing myopic concern for nurture, understood primarily as schooling and instruction and undergirded by increasingly vague pluralistic theologies, will not be adequate for framing the future of religious education. Today we face an extremely radical problem which only revolution can address. We must now squarely face the fundamental question: Will our children have faith?

The Shaking of the Foundations

The roots of our problem go back to the turn of the century and a joke: "When is a school not a school?" The answer: "When it is a Sunday school!" Coming when it did, this characteristic comment triggered a reaction throughout mainline Protestantism. A new generation of leaders, in what was commonly referred to as religious education, emerged. They were embarrassed by the Sunday school and impressed by the emerging public school system with its new understandings of child development and pedagogy. The Sunday school, they believed, was outmoded and needed to be replaced. The times, they concluded, called for both the birth of a new church school (modeled after the public schools) and the introduction of religious instruction into the nation's common schools. Thus, in 1903 the Religious Education Association was founded with the dual purposes of inspiring the religious forces of our country with an educational ideal and the educational forces with a religious one.

The church school envisioned by these women and men of the progressive era conformed to an image of the best in public education. A new profession was born to create and sustain the church school. Seminaries developed departments of religious education and conferred degrees, directors and ministers of religious education were employed by the churches, and denominations responded with a new educational bureaucracy The old-time people's Sunday school had begun to be transformed into the professional's church school. Soon religious education, influenced by liberal theology, was identified with church schooling and the

3

instruction of children, youth, and adults according to the methods of modern pedagogy.

Gradually the theological foundations of the religious education movement began to crumble, and by the late 40s and 50s most mainline denominations had adopted, in varying degrees, the theology of neoorthodoxy. Religious education changed its name to Christian education, but the image of the church school and religious instruction remained intact. Large educational plants modeled after modern public school architecture and equipped with the latest in educational technology were built wherever economically feasible. More professionals were hired by local churches to direct these burgeoning educational institutions attached to local churches, and denominational curriculum resources erupted as big business.

During the 60s a few significant voices spoke out for a broader understanding of Christian education—Randolph Crump Miller, D. Campbell Wyckoff, C. Ellis Nelson, Robert Havighurst, Roger Shinn, Ross Snyder, Rachel Henderlite, and Sara Little, to name a few. They boldly attempted to make the case that effective programs of Christian education needed to be planned in the light of the total mission and ministry of the church. They acknowledged that the church teaches most significantly through nurture in a worshiping, witnessing community of faith, and they clearly explained that explicit instruction in the church schools was only a small part of Christian education. Nevertheless, even they placed special emphasis on the church school and on instruction; few heard their call for a broader perspective.

We now find ourselves in the 70s with the foundations of neo-orthodoxy eroded, and seemingly unable to envision any significant alternative to the church school. Rachel Henderlite reminds us that we can't go home again, C. Ellis Nelson emphasizes religious socialization, and Randolph Crump Miller shifts his attention to theological foundations. A few voices, like Edward A. Powers in his book, *Signs of Shalom*, repeat the earlier call for a broader understanding of Christian education and an attempt to provide a new theological foundation. Nevertheless, local church folk still ask for help in revitalizing their church schools without any particular theological foundation. A host of panaceas in the form of methodologies or new variations on the church school, such as family clusters, flourish for a time and denominations still strive to produce better curriculum resources.

Vast amounts of money continue to be spent on teacher training, educational technology, and buildings. Numerous colleges have developed degree programs in Christian education to supply churches with economical semiprofessionals to save and revitalize their church schools. Denominations develop public relations compaigns to save the church school, and salvation by a new curriculum is still promised. A few reversals in past trends, or even a leveling off in the attendance decline, give people new hope, but still our educational ministries flounder. A broader perspective from which to evaluate, plan, and engage in Christian education is still not understood or accepted. Some continue to offer a prophetic word and preach about alternatives, but little appears to change. Why?

Will Our Children Have Faith?

I am convinced that the very foundations upon which we engage in Christian education are shaking. And while a host of builders attempt with varying degrees of success to shore them up, there is a dearth of architects engaged in designing new structures. The church's educational problem rests not in its educational program, but in the paradigm or model which undergirds its educational ministry—the agreed-upon frame of reference which guides its educational efforts.

Every field of endeavor operates out of some common frame of reference or identity. Most often we take this orientation for granted; it guides our work, helps us shape our questions, and provides us with insights for solutions to our problems. The paradigm within which we labor tells us what to do and provides us with a language to share our efforts with others.

Religious educators hold in common certain assumptions about their endeavor. The language of religious education—subject matter, what we want someone else to know—is an expression of those understandings. The set of assumptions, orientation, and frame of reference which informs us is expressed in the paradigm by which we engage in educational ministry. Since the turn of the century, in spite of nods to other possibilities, Christian educators and local churches have functioned according to a *schooling-instructional paradigm*. That is, our image of education has been founded upon some sort of a "school" as the context *and* some form of instruction as the means. Seminaries, denominational bureaucracies, educational professionals, and

6

local church lay persons have all shared this common perspective.

Within the confines of this model, a great number of imaginative, important, and relevant contributions to Christian education have been made; and a significant influence on the lives of adults, youth and children can be observed. It is only natural, therefore, that we have assured ourselves that improving the techniques and resources of schooling and instruction will continue to solve our educational problem and meet our educational needs. But, limited by a once helpful model, we have blindly and unconsciously proceeded as if there were no other possible way. Attempts to broaden that perspective, while intellectually acknowledged, are functionally resisted, and so we continue to let the schooling-instruction paradigm define our problem and establish the criteria for choosing questions to be addressed. As a result, only particular issues are acknowledged and only certain questions answered. The schooling-instructional paradigm isolates us from new possibilities while continuing to occupy most of our attention in teaching, research, practice, and resource development. To compound our difficulties, we find it functionally difficult to imagine or create any significant educational program outside it.

Of course, this is not uniquely a problem of the church. The church mirrors the society in that education in the United States operates according to a similar paradigm. Any attempt to de-school society or question the adequacy of instruction is either ignored or met with hostility. The schooling-instructional paradigm has dominated our thinking for some time, but not always. Recall that Plato, in all

Will Our Children Have Faith?

his discussions of education, gives little attention to schools. As far as Plato was concerned, it is the community that educates, by which he meant the multiplicity of formal and informal forces which influence persons.

In this century, John Dewey began his important career by assuring us that all of life educates, and that instruction in schools represents only one small part of our total education. Furthermore, he insisted that there were many forms of deliberate education. At that point Dewey was a Platonist, but late in his life, confronted by urbanization and the technological revolution, he reflected on education in American society and contended that education in the home, church, and community was no longer adequate for the day. Supported by this conclusion, he made the great twentieth-century theory jump: the school must do it. From that moment on education in the United States has been functionally coexistent with schooling and instruction. If persons are killed on the highways, we add driver education; if girls have children out of wedlock, we add sex education. No matter what the problem or need, we organize a course. Schooling and instruction have become the panaceas for all our needs. Of course our schooling and instructional methods are continually reformed, but our faith in them is never questioned.

The church, mirroring the culture, operates according to a similar paradigm, and for about the same reasons. Professional religious educators at the turn of the century didn't feel that the old Sunday school, with its dependence upon other related institutions—home, country, church, and public school—could do the job. Thus, they focused their attention on a reformed church school that could do the job by itself. Consequently, no matter what the church's needs,

8

our typical solution has been to develop courses of instruction for the church's school.

I contend that we have become victimized by this schooling-instructional understanding of religious education and imprisoned by its implications. As long as it informs our labors, significant alternatives will have difficulty being born or sustained.

While admitting that learning takes place in many ways, church education has functionally equated the context of education with schooling and the means of education with formal instruction. The public schools have provided us with our model of education, and insights from secular pedagogy and psychology have been our guides. A church school with teachers, subject matter, curriculum resources, supplies, equipment, age-graded classes, classrooms, and, where possible, a professional church educator as administrator, has been the norm. All this must change.

ANOMALIES

While some paradigm is necessary if we are to engage in any significant endeavor, any particular frame of reference may limit our awareness of new possibilities and act as a barrier to alternative understandings. Unaware of the character and limitations of the paradigm which informs our efforts, we are in danger of missing the anomalies—irregularities or deviations—that question our frame of reference. Even as we operate according to some agreed-upon understandings, it is important to be aware of the

9

anomalies that question its viability. Of course, anomalies are not easily spotted or acknowledged.

Jerome Bruner once carried out an experiment in which he took a deck of cards and flashed them on a screen at differing rates of speed. In that deck he had placed a red ace of spades and a black four of hearts and at first no one saw the unusual cards. Rather, they corrected them and reported a black four of spades and red ace of hearts. Some sensed that something was not right—that an anomaly was present—but even when Bruner flashed the cards slowly, one at a time, some persons couldn't spot any anomalies. In a similar way, assumptions can limit our awareness, and while assumptions help us to achieve a stable consensus, they are typically conservative and so make it difficult to alter our understandings and ways, even in the face of compelling evidence that we should do so.

This, I contend, is the problem we face in Christian education today. We have accepted the assumptions of the schooling-instructional paradigm and missed the anomalies which make it no longer viable for our educational mission and ministry.

THE SMALL CHURCH

Following the lead of the public school movement, religious educators focused their attention on church schools—new educational institutions. Soon these institutions were divorced from the people and from church life, and rarely were they able to meet the needs of any but our larger, sophisticated, suburban churches.

The Shaking of the Foundations

Recently, I discovered the large, important world of the small church. As a professional church educator, I had often ignored these thousands of small churches and, like other Church educators, I had gotten used to talking about educational plants, supplies, equipment, curriculum, teacher training, age-graded classes, and learning centers with individualized instruction. Lately, I've been confronted by churches which share a pastor and will probably never be able to afford the services of a professional church educator. At best they have a couple of small inadequate rooms attached to their church building, no audiovisual equipment, few supplies, an inadequate number of prospective teachers, and not enough students for age-graded classes. The Sunday church schools in these small mainline Protestant churches are sick—in part because they have tried to become modern church schools and failed. The Sunday school "statistics board" in the front of their churches dramatizes their situation and denominational programs, most of which they are unable to use, and creates feelings of inadequacy and failure.

Depression results from the realization that the great majority of Protestant churches have less than two hundred members. Many of these churches have nevertheless faithfully striven to turn their Sunday schools into church schools and have failed. The severity of the problem is great. One anomaly, the schooling-instruction paradigm, can be seen in the realization that most small churches will never be able to mount up or support the sort of schooling and instruction upon which religious education has been founded since the turn of the century.

Will Our Children Have Faith?

Also consider the numerous ethnic churches in our country. At one time I was the liaison person for the United Church Board for Homeland Ministries with our churches in Hawaii, and on one of my visits I met with the members of a number of small native Hawaiian churches. They still called their church schools Sunday schools, although through the years they had obediently and faithfully striven to develop a Christian education program like that recommended by the church's educational professionals. They struggled to raise money to build classrooms, they bought the denomination's curriculum resources, and they sent their people to teacher-training workshops and lab schools. And yet attendance continued to drop, teachers were difficult to secure and, more seriously, the faith was not being adequately transmitted or sustained.

They asked me why they were failing, and I was stumped. They were doing everything we had suggested and still they were unsuccessful. In desperation, I asked them to tell me about the days when they were succeeding. They explained that a number of churches gathered each Sunday evening for a luau. Young and old came together to sing hymns, tell the Gospel story, witness to their faith, discuss their lives as Christians, minister to each other's needs, eat, and have fellowship. They did almost everything natural to their culture except dance, which we had taught them was "immoral." When they finished describing their old educational programs, I could think of nothing but to suggest they return to having luaus, knowing that those committed to schooling and instruction would think me mad.

The Shaking of the Foundations

While most of our Protestant churches are small, some seventy percent of all church members reside in churches of three hundred or more people, and one might conjecture that the schooling-instruction paradigm is viable in these churches. During the last few years I have visited a number of large dynamic church schools directed by qualified, creative, professional staffs. And I have found that there are quite a few churches where the dream of "the perfect" church school has been actualized. In these churches, most of the teachers are well-trained and many have developed their own exemplary curriculum resources. The educational plants, equipment, supplies, and organization would make many a public school envious. Attendance at church school has not significantly diminished, and there is still enthusiasm for their many innovative programs. And yet, in almost every case they have evaluated their achievements and found them lacking. The modern church school at its very best is less than adequate for our day. The reason is another anomaly in the schooling-instructional paradigm.

During the first third of this century an "ecology"—a pattern of relations between organisims and their environment—of institutions was consciously engaged in religious education. First, there was the community. Life in any typical American town nurtured persons in a Protestant ethos and atmosphere. Others—Roman Catholics, Jews, and others—lived and were nurtured in their own homogeneous communities.

Second, the family was basically secure, extended, and stable. There was little mobility; both parents were frequently home and shared family life together. And if not living under the same roof, relatives lived nearby and were in continuous interaction with the family. Divorce was less frequent, few women worked outside the home, and families were larger. There were few one-parent families and almost no interfaith marriages. Most persons were nurtured, married, and died within a hundred miles of their birth. In this environment, the family provided a natural setting and made a significant contribution to a person's religious education.

Third, most public schools were Protestant parochial schools. From the daily morning ritual of Bible reading (King James Version) and the Lord's prayer (with a Protestant benediction) to the textbooks complete with moral and religious lessons (The McGuffey Readers), children acquired general foundational Protestant religious education. Roman Catholics, in turn, supported their own parochial school system to educate their children.

Fourth, there was the church. The typical church was a community neighborhood congregation where all ages knew each other and regularly interacted. Many hours were spent at the church, not only in worship but in a variety of social activities. Here persons were socialized in the shared understandings and ways of their particular denomination.

Fifth, a great number of popular religious periodicals provided the major source of "entertainment" and religious education in the home.

Sixth and last, the Sunday school completed this ecology of institutions deliberately engaged in religious education. (Roman Catholics depended on courses in religion taught by nuns in the parochial schools.) The Sunday school was especially important in that it was a lay-directed organization where women could play a significant leadership role.

It provided an intergenerational setting where persons could celebrate Easter, Christmas, Thanksgiving, Missionary Day, and Dedication Day. Always concerned about community, celebration, the religious affections, and the biblical story, these Sunday schools included plays and musicals, games, hikes and hunts, homecomings and family gatherings, parties and picnics, social service projects and community activities.

These six institutions intentionally worked together to produce an effective educational ecology.

But now an anomaly is found in our changing situation, for today most communities (especially those in which we find our larger churches) are heterogeneous. A pluralism of religious and secular persuasions interact and compete, and no longer can the community be counted upon to transmit a particular set of understandings and ways.

The family has changed also. Families are smaller and children often lack any significant direct interaction with the grandparents and relatives. Increasingly, both parents work outside the home, actual or functional one-parent families are on the increase, interfaith marriages are common, and the average family moves frequently and is typically without roots. Many functions of the family once carried out in the home have been assumed by the society. Day-care centers for children, retirement homes for the aging, recreation organizations for youth, and hospitals for the care of the sick are but a few examples of these now transferred functions.

The public school is now the religiously neutral institution intended by the Constitution, where at best religion can be taught *about* and studied objectively. Fewer Roman Catholics now send their children to parochial schools.

Will Our Children Have Faith?

Today the church is rarely the center of people's social and community life; it is not uncommon for families to go away on weekends and find their numerous needs met in a diversity of secular groups. Television and an array of mass secular media have replaced religious publications.

So we are left with a church school (or parish Confraternity of Christian Doctrine (C.C.D.) program) struggling to do alone what it took an ecology of six institutions to do in the past. It cannot be done, but the schooling-instructional paradigm ignores this changing situation.

THE HIDDEN CURRICULUM

For a variety of reasons, the schooling-instructional paradigm inadequately addresses the educational needs of both the small and large church. More important, however, is an anomaly in the schooling-instructional paradigm that affects them both; namely the manner in which this paradigm eliminates the processes of religious socialization from the concern and attention of church educators and parishioners.

By socialization I mean all those formal and informal influences through which persons acquire their understandings and ways of living. For example, I have friends who have one child. The mother is a professional journalist who travels a great deal, and the father has willingly performed most of the parenting functions for their young daughter. On one occasion I observed the little girl playing house. Noticing that she was holding a doll, I inquired, "Who are you?" "I'm the father," she explained. "Oh, where is the mother?" I asked. "Well, she's away writing a story." That is socialization. No one intentionally sat down and taught this young girl that fathers take care of children and mothers work; she learned it without a school or instruction.

Education correctly understood is not identical with schooling. It is an aspect of socialization involving all deliberate, systematic and sustained efforts to transmit or evolve knowledge, attitudes, values, behaviors, or sensibilities. The history of religious education, therefore, needs to include the family, public schools, community ethos, religious literature, and church life. Schooling, on the other hand, is only one specific and very limited form of education. The schooling-instructional paradigm has made this small part into the whole and, by accepting this understanding, we have typically forgotten that even in the school the "hidden curriculum" of socialization is at work influencing what is learned.

Recently, I have been engaged in the study of schools and sex-role stereotyping. While visiting an elementary school, the principal thought I should visit a class using a new unit on human sexuality. What amazed him was my greater interest in walking through the halls. He asked to join me in my walk, and we observed the following: Female teachers go into both the boys' and girls' rooms while male teachers only go into the boys' room; girls and boys are encouraged to play very different sorts of games; teachers correct or punish boys and girls in significantly different ways; there are no male teachers in the kindergarten and no female administrators; photographs in classrooms consistently have men and women in sex-defined roles. Later we talked and I tried to explain that no intentional course of study could adequately counter the hidden curriculum of that school. Indeed, it was daily life in that school which primarily affected persons' understandings and ways.

The same can be said about the church and the church school, but the schooling-instructional paradigm tends to isolate the process of socialization from our consideration. Because the informal hidden curriculum in our churches is often more influential than the formal curriculum of our church schools, the schooling-instruction paradigm will always be less than inadequate for the evaluation and planning of Christian education. For example: Once I taught a senior high class in worship, in which we learned that the offering was a symbolic, communal act in response to the Gospel of the people's intentions and commitments for life in the world. The class decided that the church's offering of money once a year for racial justice did not meet the criteria of an offering, and they suggested asking the congregation to place on the altar an offering of signed fair housing pledge cards. After a few minutes of discussion at a board meeting, the church's adult leaders turned down the suggestion on political and economic grounds. Where was the more significant learning, in the church school class or at the board meeting?

We can teach about equality in our church schools, but if our language in worship excludes women, if positions of influence and importance are held only by men or those from upper socioeconomic classes, or if particular races are either implicitly or explicitly excluded from membership, a different lesson is learned. Naming rooms in churches after wealthy donors may only teach children that the Christian life is one of gaining affluence. If we organize the church so that whenever time or talents are requested it is for serving the institutional needs, people are not apt to learn that the

Christian life is one of mission in the world. And so it goes. As long as we operate by a schooling-instruction paradigm numerous significant influences will be ignored.

THE WRONG QUESTIONS

We continue to accept the established as real; we assume that if we know more about teaching and learning, we can solve our educational problems. Faced by curricular needs we turn to technology and neglect new ways of being together. Faced with nonresponsive students, we turn to psychology to understand and control behavior instead of reflecting on the meaning of two persons in relationship. Confronted by difficulties in classroom discussion, cooperation, or morale, we consider the latest group-dynamics technique instead of rethinking the nature of community. When facing new problems we typically respond by focusing even more sharply on formal teaching and learning, believing that it is possible, with new knowledge and techniques, to build a workable school for the church, train an adequate number of capable teachers, and provide more useful curriculum resources for quality church education. In bondage to this inadequate understanding, we interpret any small success or reversal of existing negative trends in church schooling as a confirmation of the old paradigm's validity. This anomaly in the schooling-instructional paradigm, therefore, relates to the sources of influence which inform its life.

We have permitted the behavioral sciences to give us a source of false optimism. We have assumed that the more we know about people and learning, the more effective will be our educational efforts. We have believed that if stages of thinking can be identified, then both resources and teaching techniques to answer all our educational needs can be designed. However, our deepest problems may be of a different nature. Perhaps we need to rethink and reshape the institutions within which people dwell, and begin struggling with what it means to be Christian together.

Another example results from the unfortunate fact that the schooling-instructional paradigm encourages adults to be with children in ways that assert their power over them. The language of teaching, learning, behavorial objectives, and subject matter tend to produce a mind-set that results in the tendency to inflict on children adult ways of being in the world. It is difficult for us simply to be with the neophyte in song, worship, prayer, storytelling, service, reflection, and fellowship. We always seem to want to do something to or for them so they will be like us or like what we would like to be.

But education grounded in Christian faith cannot be a vehicle for control; it must encourage an equal sharing of life in community, a cooperative opportunity for reflection on the meaning and significance of life. Surely we must share our understandings and ways with children, but we also must remember that they have something to bring to us and that what we bring to children is always under God's judgment. Of course, it is easier to impose than reflect, easier to instruct than share, easier to act than to interact. It is important, however, to remember that to be with a child in Christian ways means self-control more than child-control.

To be Christian is to ask: What can I bring to another?

Not: What do I want that person to know or be? It means being open to learn from another person (even a child) as well as to share one's understandings and ways. To speak of schooling and instruction leads us in other directions and to other conclusions. Should we not ask: Is schooling and instruction in a Christian community necessary for education? Or is living as a Christian with others inherently educational? If we attend to being Christian with others, need we attend to schooling and instruction? By focusing on schooling and instruction, we have ignored these issues and questions that are so important for Christian faith.

RELIGION OR FAITH

We have too easily linked the ways of secular education with religion. Dependence upon the practice, rhetoric, and norms of secular psychology and pedagogy is risky business. Perhaps there is something unique about education in religious communities. That uniqueness is made clear in the last anomaly I wish to mention.

This anomaly surfaces in the awareness of what purposes schooling and instruction best serve. Recall the question asked in the Gospel according to St. Luke: "When the Son of Man comes will he find faith on earth?" (Luke 18:8). Surely he will find religion (institutions, creeds, documents, artifacts, and the like), but he may not find faith. Faith is deeply personal, dynamic, ultimate. Religion, however, is faith's expression. For example, religion is concerned about institutions (churches), documents, state-

21

ments of belief (Bible and theology), and our convictions and moral codes. Religion is important, but not ultimately important. Educationally, religion is a means not an end; faith is the only end. Faith, therefore, and not religion, must become the concern of Christian education.

The anomaly of the schooling-instruction paradigm is found in its natural and primary concern with religion. You can teach about religion, but you cannot teach people faith. Thus, this paradigm places Christian education in the strange position of making secondary matters primary. Teaching people *about* Christianity is not very important. Religion at best is an expression of someone's faith which, under proper conditions, can lead others to faith. Bach wrote the "B Minor Mass" as an expression of his faith, and I have faith in part because I am moved to faith whenever I hear it. However, knowing all about the "B Minor Mass" is not to be confused with having faith; indeed, one can know all about it and not be Christian at all.

It appears that as Christian faith has diminished, the schooling-instructional paradigm has encouraged us to busy ourselves with teaching *about* Christian religion. As our personal commitment to Christ has lapsed, many church persons have turned for solace to teaching children what the Bible says, what happened in the history of the church, what we believe, and what is right and wrong. Sometimes, even when the school has succeeded, it has only produced educated atheists. For many today, Christian religion as taught in our church schools stands between them and God. The schooling-instructional paradigm easily leads us into thinking that we have done our jobs if we teach children all *about* Christianity.

There is a great difference between learning about the

Bible and living as a disciple of Jesus Christ. We are not saved by our knowledge, our beliefs, or our worship in the church; just as we are not saved by our actions or our religion. We are saved by the anguish and love of God, and to live according to that truth is to have faith.

Faith cannot be taught by any method of instruction; we can only teach religion. We can know about religion, but we can only expand in faith, act in faith, live in faith. Faith can be inspired within a community of faith, but it cannot be given to one person by another. Faith is expressed, transformed, and made meaningful by persons sharing their faith in an historical, tradition-bearing community of faith. An emphasis on schooling and instruction makes it too easy to forget this truth. Indeed, the schooling-instructional paradigm works against our necessary primary concern for the faith of persons. It encourages us to teach about Christian religion by turning our attention to Christianity as expressed in documents, doctrines, history, and moral codes. No matter what the rhetoric of our purposes, the schooling-instructional paradigm, modeled after modern psychology and pedagogy, leads us to focus on religion rather than faith. If for no other reason than this, the schooling-instructional paradigm needs to be questioned.

A BANKRUPTCY

I have concluded, therefore, that the schooling-instructional paradigm is bankrupt. An alternative paradigm, not merely an alternative educational program, is needed. But that is easier said than done. Our dilemma is exemplified in

Will Our Children Have Faith?

a Sufi story about a person who, having looted a city, was trying to sell an exquisite rug. "Who will give me a hundred pieces of silver for this rug?" he cried. After the sale was completed, a comrade approached the seller and asked, "Why did you not ask more for that priceless rug?" "Is there a number larger than one hundred?" asked the seller.

Until we can imagine an alternative to our present schooling-instructional paradigm, our efforts at Christian education will be inadequate and increasingly ineffective. However, a new paradigm cannot be created in a vacuum. Christian education is dependent upon theological underpinnings, a fact that we have forgotten on occasion; relying, rather, upon insights from philosophy, the social sciences, or general education. Before we can explore an alternative paradigm, we must reflect on our theological convictions, so to that task we turn. But first a word of hope.

Unless hope is aroused and alive there is little reason to struggle with an alternative paradigm. Remember, therefore, that hope has its foundations in dissatisfactions with the present. Hope is founded upon the death of the old and the birth of the new. There are those who are troubled by death, the unknown, the new, but the Christian faith finds hope for tomorrow in the destruction of old ways and understandings.

Questioning our schooling-instructional paradigm provides us with a significant opportunity to rethink what we are about in religious education. It is not wise to depend on our own short, unreflective pasts or on our current endeavors to provide insight for the future, for when we do, we too easily accept the established as real. The future is in our imaginations and with God. In that conviction is our hope. As we celebrate the death of past understandings, we go forth, as pilgrims in faith, in search of new ones to support our educational ministry. We affirm the need to grapple with the radical question: Will our children have faith?

CHAPTER TWO

Beginning and Ending with Faith

Religious educators must find a more dynamic theology for the emerging age or resign themselves to the inevitable eclipse of their movement in the American church.

H. Shelton Smith

A CHALLENGE confronts us, for not only do we face the crisis of a bankrupt paradigm, we face a corresponding crisis in our theological foundations. Inevitably, that places us in a particularly acute situation, for Christian education is dependent upon the theological underpinnings which judge and inspire its efforts. We would be foolish to attempt the description of an alternative paradigm without first exploring some theological issues.

Today this task is complicated by the variety of theological positions which vie for our attention: conservative, evangelical, liberal, new Reformation, charismatic, third-world, black, feminist, hermeneutical, process, and eschatological. More serious is the theological agnosticism, confusion, and pluralism that exists in most local churches and which religious educators have tended to accept too easily. It is one thing for theologians to argue divergent positions within an agreed-upon historical understanding of Christian faith, but the local church cannot develop an adequate educational ministry when the pluralism with which it lives lacks agreement on theological essentials. Indeed, the church cannot proceed to develop an educational ministry without a clear, acknowledged theological foundation. A unity of theology and education is a necessity, not a luxury.

HISTORIC ROOTS

The first two decades of this century witnessed the emergence of religious education as a major movement in American mainline Protestantism, and interest in it eclipsed every other aspect of church life. Influenced by liberal modes of theological thought from the previous century, the social Gospel, and the progressive educational theories of John Dewey, religious education had a mind and soul. At no point in American Protestantism did the social interpretation of the Gospel root itself more strongly than in the religious education movement. George Albert Coe's book, *A Social Theory of Religious Education* (Arno Press, 1969) is a landmark in our history and a work of continuing significance.

A number of liberal theological presuppositions laid the foundations and gave vitality to the religious education movement. With regard to human nature, they emphasized a person's capacity for good. The significance of personal experience was affirmed. Sin was understood primarily as error or limitation, both of which could be addressed by education. A strong emphasis on moral education accompanied this liberal understanding of persons. Optimistic about the destiny of the human race, the kingdom of God was given a this-worldly interpretation. Convinced that with proper education persons could contribute to the building of God's kingdom within the natural historical process, the liberals emphasized the imminence of God and his social kingdom. Religion and ethics were made inseparable. Coupled with convictions of the social Gospel movement, religious education affirmed education's important role in the salvation of society.

However, history never remains fixed. Social situations change, and with them our theological positions. In the 30s a new theological voice was heard. Liberalism had reached its zenith and neo-orthodoxy was born as a necessary corrective to its extremes. Personal experience was now to be depreciated while the centrality of the Scriptures and the authority of the biblical revelation was announced. Sin was identified as more than human ignorance; it was the natural corruption of the will. Salvation could no longer be understood as a product of education, and the expectation that we humans could build the kingdom of God was dispelled. Instead, God's kingdom was understood as a judgment over all human achievements. Countering liberalism's belief in the social self, neo-orthodoxy affirmed the individuality of persons, each of whom lives under the judgment and grace of God. Conversion was once again emphasized as necessary for salvation, and the church was called to its uniqueness as a community of the saints set apart from the world.

The impact of neo-orthodoxy on the church's educational ministry was great. Religious education was transformed into Christian education. As a "johnny-come-lately" to this theological reversal, I have always been troubled by the way in which the corresponding truths in liberalism and neo-orthdoxy became estranged. Christian education, I contend, paid a great price for the church's inability to reconcile and unite these two complementary (often paradoxical) theological positions.

From my readings of Scripture, liberal theology correctly affirmed God's indwelling presence and action in the world process. History is intentional and directional and God is perpetually and universally acting in the world of nature, persons, and society. Neo-orthodoxy, on the other hand, rightly reclaimed God's transcendence. God acts in history but is not to be identified with history. We do not fully comprehend who God is or how God works, but God does reveal himself in God's historical actions. Society and persons are fallen, and God acts over against his fallen creation to redeem it. Nevertheless, God also acts in and through the lives of persons and nations to do his will. Liberal theology emphasized the historical personage of Jesus, his human example and ethical importance, but ignored his divine nature as Jesus Christ and his importance as God's saving action in the world. Liberal theology correctly affirmed the importance of personal experience but neglected the authority of Scripture and tradition which both inspires and judges all personal experience. Liberalism rightly affirmed the social self and the social nature of the Gospel and salvation, while neo-orthodoxy rightly reminded us of the individual converted soul's importance.

A DECISION

Now once again we who are responsible for Christian education in the church are confronted with a crucial decision: What theological orientation will inform our labors? The religious education movement was an offspring of liberal theology, and when neo-orthodoxy emerged, its influence was felt. H. Shelton Smith, caught in the midst of this struggle between liberalism and neo-orthodoxy, correctly reminded the church in his important book, *Faith and Nurture*, of the essential unity between education and theology. He also wisely sought to build a bridge between liberalism's concern for the social order and neo-orthodoxy's concern for the tradition. But at the time (1940s) there was no acceptable theology to hold these two positions together, and his message went unheard. Today, liberation theology makes possible a synthesis of these two historic theological movements. Moreover, liberation theology makes possible important coalitions between Roman Catholic and Protestant (witness the ecumenical character of its adherents); liberals and conservatives (witness the continuing concerns of the World Council of Churches and the new evangelical witness in the Chicago Declaration); majorities and minorities (witness the number of theological books written from a black, feminist, third-world, and Anglo-white perspective).

Therefore, while each of the numerous current theological positions vying for attention offers valuable insights, I contend that liberation theology provides the most helpful theological system for Christian education today. This conviction is founded upon my belief that liberation theology makes possible the long-avoided and essential unification of neo-orthodoxy's concern for the historic Christian tradition with liberalism's concern for justice and the social order. In the past our educational efforts have been informed by one or the other, but now a new synthesis is possible. Liberation theologians—Herzog, Cone, Ruether, Gutierrez, Russell, Roberts, Alves, and others—may differ, but they all share common methods, perspectives, and themes. In terms of method, liberation theology understands theology as critical reflection on the activity of God in history. Theology is drawn from our human experience and our common search for the right questions as well as the right answers. This form of practical theology brings action and reflection together; it unites Scripture, tradition, and experience.

Liberation theology also shares three common perspectives on the experience of God in history. First is the biblical promise of liberation. God is the one who sets people free, and the Gospel announces the good news of liberation. God is biased toward the marginal people—the have-nots, the oppressed, the hurt, the outsiders. Christ has set and is setting the captives free. Secondly, life is understood as centered in history and is changing and changeable. That is, life is a series of events moving the world in the direction God intends. Liberation theology asserts that we have hope because we have a memory of God's past acts in history; and we have purpose because God has given us a vision of the future God intends. Third, salvation is a social event in the present, not an escape from history but an engagement within history.

Finally, the uniting theme of liberation theology is the humanization of persons and institutions. The continuing struggle of the faithful Christian is centered in the call to act accordingly. Liberation theology affirms that we are responsible for shaping history and that we can join God in God's history-making. Education as action/reflection can play a significant role in helping us to live, individually and corporately, under the judgment and inspiration of the Gospel to the end that God's will be done and God's community (kingdom) comes.

Within this general understanding of liberation theology, however, there are specific theological issues especially important for the church's educational mission and ministry which need to be addressed. What follows is not a theological system or a theology for Christian education, but rather reflections on a series of theological issues. Like most theological statements they will be incomplete and perhaps slanted, but every generation is called upon to reflect on its historic tradition and to interpret that tradition for its own day. To respond to that call is to decide what issues must be addressed and hence emphasized. I have chosen those which I believe are most crucial for the church's educational mission and ministry. They are: the nature of God, revelation, and authority; the nature of persons, conversion, and nurture; the nature of the church, discipleship, and individual-social life. To these issues we turn now. My responses are not meant to be complete or definitive, but they are meant to provide a theological framework for religious education and foundations for the development of an alternative to the schooling-instructional paradigm.

Beginning and Ending with Faith

GOD

(I am troubled as to how to speak of God. He/she seems right, but perhaps only the word God should be used. I do not want to distort the nature of God nor ignore the justice due those who are left out and estranged by masculine language. Forgive, therefore, my lack of imagination and read each "he" as intended; that is, as pointing to God, inclusive of all those characteristics culturally attributed to women and/or men—the creator, liberator, and comforter of all people.)

There is only one place a theology for education can begin—with God, the God who acts and thereby discloses himself and his intentions for creation. God, in the Christian faith, refers to the *one who acts*. Over and over again the Bible emphasizes the deeds that God has done. The God of the Christian faith is a living, dynamic *will*, with purposes for the world and the power to realize them. God's will is for justice, equity, whole community, and the well-being of all. God's purposes are shaped by love using power to overcome oppression. God is a mystery and yet God reveals himself—his will, purposes, and power—in historic activity.

God is an agent. God acts in history on behalf of his coming community where justice, liberation, wholeness of life, unity, peace, and the well-being of all peoples are realized. That is the central affirmation to be made about God. It is the good news of what God has done in Jesus Christ.

The centrality of the Bible for Christian faith is derived from its record of God's activity. The Old and the New Testaments are important because they contain the story of

33

Will Our Children Have Faith?

God's actions in history and his people's attempt to understand and respond. From the biblical story, we also learn who we are and how we are to live. The historic interpretations and pronouncements of the church provide us with a continuing resource for understanding the story. Our individual and corporate experiences with God and others in history provide us with the context in which the story assumes meaning in each generation. The Bible, however, remains the source and norm of Christian faith.

Nevertheless, the written words of the Bible are not our final authority, nor are the doctrines of the church, nor are our own personal inner experiential convictions. While each provides us with one aspect of the authority upon which Christian faith is founded, it is God's historic liberating action in Jesus Christ that is the final authority and the foundation for Christian faith. In the life, death, and resurrection of Jesus Christ, God provides us with the basis for understanding, interpreting, and applying our faith story.

At the heart of our Christian faith is a story. And at the heart of Christian education must be this same story. When we evaluate our corporate lives as a community of faith, this story must judge us. Our ritual life, the experiences we have in community, and the acts we perform in the world, must be informed by this story. Unless the story is known, understood, owned, and lived, we and our children will not have Christian faith. The struggle to know, understand, interpret, live, and do God's word must be at the center of our educational mission. For too long the church and its educational ministry has supported a strange and deafening silence. We have tried to live as if the story were unimportant. Only when the Christian story of God's actions in history becomes the focus of our educational ministry will that ministry be Christian. The Bible must once again become our one and only "textbook," for in its story we come to know the actor God who creates, redeems, and sustains life in the past, present, and future. Further, when the faith community's story becomes our story, God's presence among us as historic actor becomes a part of our experience.

PERSONS

We began with God because our understanding of God is prior and because every statement about God is finally a statement about persons. We are created by God in God's image. The best way to understand ourselves, therefore, is as historical actors. The human self, like God, is an *agent*. We act through the integration of our thinking, feeling, and willing, but the self is ultimately a doer. All meaningful knowledge is for action, and our knowledge of the world is a result of our actions in the world. We know God through God's actions and through participation with God in his actions; we know others through their actions and our interactions with them; we know ourselves through our actions and interactions with others.

We are historical actors, free and determined. We live a paradoxical existence in which we shape and are shaped, influence and are influenced. The world and the historical process is the meeting place of actors.

The self as actor is not an isolated individual. Our existence is dependent upon interactions with God and other persons. The isolated individual self is a fiction, but so is the social self. To affirm only a social self is to overemphasize the role nurture and socialization play in framing us.

Will Our Children Have Faith?

To affirm only the individual self, naked and responsible before God, is to underestimate the significance of other historical actors in our lives. In truth we are corporate selves who live in a continual dynamic relationship with all others and with God. The self is constituted by its relationships; human life is essentially corporate. God created human beings with a need for community, and therefore we cannot be human or Christian alone. Community and corporate identity are not optional. We are corporate selves who have been created to relate with God and each other—with all others—in freedom and responsibility. We may misuse our freedom and deny our responsibility by trying to live unto ourselves without God and others, or against God and others, yet we are still bound together. If any one person is oppressed, hurt, denied equity and justice, or kept marginal, we are all prevented from achieving full humanness.

Our created corporate selfhood places us in an essential relationship with *all* others. Because God is in relationship with all persons, we cannot be in full community with God unless we also identify with and seek the good of *all* persons. To reach this goal it is especially important for us to be biased (as God is biased) toward the oppressed and hurt, those outside the benefit of the system—that is, toward the have-nots of this world. Our human sin is revealed in both our denial of corporate selfhood (a denial which estranges us from God, neighbor, and self) and in our apathy and sloth (a condition which results from either believing we are not called to be responsible actors in the world or believing that we are only victims of history's determining forces).

Our human sin is revealed in our willingness to withdraw from the struggle of life, and our unwillingness to accept responsibility for history. As a result we become estranged victims of history, but God in his unmerited love acted in Christ to free us for responsible history-making. No longer need we be enslaved to those powers and institutions and practices which control and ultimately work to destroy us. We are liberated in Christ for historical action consistent with the will and purposes of God. Because of God's gracious act in the crucifixion and resurrection of Jesus Christ we have the power to join God in God's history-making, and thereby to be united with God, our neighbor, and ourselves. We are saved from the corruption of our image by an action of God alone and not by education. The Christian faith is not founded upon a Gospel of good works or advanced learning, but on the good news of God's action in Jesus Christ. Christian salvation is more than enlightenment or a scheme for good living. Salvation is God-given and not something we humans achieve by moralistic or pedagogical means. At the same time salvation is not solely an individual piety related only to personal relations with God and neighbor. The Gospel is a social Gospel, a worldly Gospel, or no Gospel at all.

Individually and corporately, we need to be converted to true freedom—freedom to act with God in history on behalf of liberation, justice, peace, unity, wholeness, community, and the well-being of all peoples.

In the not-too-distant past the church placed an emphasis on growth and social change through a gradual evolutionary process. Optimistic about the improvement of the race and social progress, we placed our emphasis on nurture. We neglected human nature and the need for radical change in our lives. The Gospel's call is to repentance. Human existence is in contradiction to God's community. We cannot do

Will Our Children Have Faith?

God's will through our own doing, nor can we build God's coming community. God will bring in God's community in God's good time, but God also calls us to join him in his community-building.

Historically, Christian education has vacillated between a concern for conversion and a concern for nurture. With the birth of the religious education movement, nurture through teaching became the dominant underlying purpose. The acquisition of faith was understood in terms of nurture and growth which functionally correspond to a gradual process of schooling. Support for this position was located in a single phrase in Horace Bushnell's *Christian Nurture* (Yale University Press, 1966). A child is to grow up as a Christian and never know himself or herself as being otherwise. This dictum may have made sense when it referred to the children of the saints, who were to be nurtured in a church whose membership was restricted to the saints and their offspring. But I contend that the church can no longer surrender to the illusion that child nurture, in and of itself, can or will rekindle the fire of Christian faith in persons or in the church.

We have expected too much of nurture, for at its very best, nurture makes possible institutional incorporation. We can nurture persons into institutional religion, but not into mature Christian faith. The Christian faith by its very nature demands conversion. We cannot gradually educate persons through instruction in schools to be Christian. Of course, persons need to be and can be nurtured into a community's faith and life. There is a basic need to belong to and identify with a faithful community, to own its story as our story, and to have our religious affections nourished.

But persons also need, if they are to grow in faith, to be

aided and encouraged to judge, inquire, question, and even to doubt that faith; to be given the opportunity to experiment with and reflect upon alternatives; and to learn what it means to commit their lives to causes and persons. Only after an intellectual struggle with our community's faith and with an honest consideration of alternatives can a person truly say "I believe,"—and thereby achieve personal Christian identity. Only then, I contend, can a person live the radical, political, economic, social life of the Christian in the world.

Conversion, I believe, is best understood as this radical turning from "faith given" (through nurture) to "faith owned." Conversion is radical because it implies ownership and the corresponding transformation of our lives. It implies a reorientation in our thinking, feeling, and willing; a moving from indifference or one form of piety to another. That is why conversion historically is only rarely a singular emotional outburst, a once-and-for-all dramatic occasion which can be dated and described. Rather, conversion is more typically a process by which persons are nurtured in a community's faith (the religion of the heart), go through the despair of doubt and the intellectual quest for understanding (the religion of the head), and at last, in late adolescence or early adulthood, experience illumination, certainty, and identity. In retrospect, most persons who achieve this mature conversion identify their early faith as inadequate and their earlier experiences of emotional conversion into the community's beliefs, attitudes, and values as insignificant.

Conversion, however, is never an isolated event devoid of all elements of nurture. Nurture and conversion are a unified whole. Neither those who nurture persons into church membership nor those who nurture persons into the acceptance of the church's dogma have taken seriously the relationship between nurture and conversion.

An example may help to explain my understanding of conversion as a reorientation of the soul, a deliberate turning from indifference or an earlier form of piety to passionate commitment to a new way of life. The life I would like to examine is that of Horace Bushnell, partly because he seems to have wanted to replace conversion with nurture, and partly because his experience is typical of almost every religious leader and saint in the history of the church. Bushnell was nurtured by religious parents in a nineteenth-century New England Congregational church. At seventeen, during a revival, he experienced a deep flow of religious feeling—"the Lord in his tender mercy led me to Jesus and saved my soul." At twenty-one he entered Yale College where his earlier religious fervor dulled and his skepticism grew. His mother hoped that he would prepare for the ministry, but Bushnell left Yale and went from teaching to journalism to law—all the time struggling with his doubts and trying to intellectualize his faith.

A few years later he returned to Yale as a tutor, only to find his pupils awaiting his words on faith. His inability to speak on the subject tormented him. He realized that he had substituted thought for everything else and, through his attempts to create a religion of the head, had pushed faith away. In prayer, he confessed to God his despair and his willingness to trust. The result was the clearing of doubt, a new enlightenment or illumination, and a commitment to enter the ministry. This later experience Bushnell describes as his true conversion to Christian faith, thereby discrediting his earlier conversion and the significance of his earlier religious experience.

Neither the pietist who has no commitment to the struggle for justice and righteousness in the world of institutional life, nor the social activist who has no personal commitment to Christ, are truly converted into mature Christian faith. True conversion—authentic Christian life—is personal and social life lived on behalf of God's will in the political, social, and economic world. The converted life is a revolutionary existence over against the status quo, a life committed to a vision of God's coming community of liberation, justice, peace, whole community, and the well-being of all people. We cannot be nurtured into such life—not in this world. Every culture strives to socialize persons to live in harmony with life as it is. The culture calls upon its religious institutions to bless the status quo and its religious educational institutions to nurture persons into an acceptance of it.

God calls his people to be signs of Shalom, the vanguard of God's coming community, a community of cultural change. To reach the conviction that such countercultural life is our Christian vocation, and to be enabled to live such a corporate existence in but not of the world, necessitates conversion as well as nurture.

Once again we need to understand that both conversion and nurture have a place in religious education if such education is to be Christian. Our sole concern for nurture has contributed to our losing both an evangelical power and a social dynamic. While rejecting a sterile revivalism, we constructed a false evangelism through nurture. Christian education for conversion means helping persons to see that they are called, not only to believe the church's affirmation that Jesus is the Christ but to commit their lives to live as his apostles and disciples in the world.

Persons, as corporate selves and historical actors, are in need of both nurture and conversion. The church's educational ministry must be founded upon this awareness.

CHURCH AND SOCIETY

One Christian is no Christian, for we cannot be Christian alone—we are created for community.

The church is best understood as a creation of God, a community of corporate social agents called to bear witness individually and corporately in word and deed to God's intention for human life, that is, to be a radical community for others, a countercultural community biased toward and acting with God on behalf of the oppressed, the hurt, the poor, the have-nots, the marginal people of the world.

The church can never exist for itself; it is never an end, only a means. Its mission, its end, is to be a community where Christian faith is proclaimed, experienced, understood, lived, and acted upon in history. But the church, while a saved community which bears the message of salvation, is also a fallen institution which often lives for itself.

A few months ago a group of my students and I engaged in a research project on rites of initiation in Protestant religious communities. Through the anthropological method of participant-observation we studied a large number of diverse groups. When we completed our work, we were forced to create a typology for rites of initiation: namely, rites of institutional incorporation and rites of faith commitment. In spite of the rhetoric of all groups that faith was their goal, we discovered that most mainline Protestant churches were primarily concerned with institutional incorporation and survival.

For example, confirmation classes were typically called membership classes, preparation centered on denominational polity, history, practice, financial support, participation in congregational life, and attendance at worship. The ritual itself had two sorts of questions. The first dealt with questions concerning faith and the second with institutional commitment. In every case we discovered that the leader of the ritual behaved in preferential ways toward the latter. One set of field notes after another disclosed that the faith questions were asked quickly, and answered in a similar manner. The minister then paused, looked the candidates in the eyes, spoke very slowly and listened very carefully for their reply to the questions on institutional loyalty. Is there any doubt which questions were considered more important? Also, when adults and parents were asked if they would be upset if their children decided not to be confirmed or baptized they typically said yes. But when asked why, they all replied that they would be lost as church members. No one expressed concern for their children's souls or faith.

Institutionally we may be less than Christian, still we are created by God for life in community. Our understanding of the Christian faith can never be individualistic. Christian life is to be lived in and for the community of God. Too often we have led persons to a life of mere inwardness or personal piety, thus blessing the existing social, political, and economic order regardless of the injustices they may perpetuate. The covenant of God's people with the Lord of history entails responsibility for the total character of society. Any restriction of religion to the immediate relation between an individual and God is a denial of the Christian story, which calls for the transformation of the whole of life. To believe that institutions will take care of themselves if individuals have personal faith is folly.

It is difficult to be or become a Christian when everyone claims the name. The Christian faith necessitates a converted radical community of faith within which to live and grow; a servant community which seeks the good of others, acts for the liberation of all persons, and aids us all to resist private gain in the search for corporate selfhood.

We are *not* called to be incorporated into the church as one institution among others. God intends that the church be a *unique* witnessing community of faith, a converted, pilgrim people living under the judgment and inspiration of the Gospel to the end that God's will is done and God's community comes. The church is called to be a community of corporate selves interacting with each other and the world as an expression of their commitment to the Lord of history.

We have sometimes neglected the church as God's chosen people, a community of radical Christian faith, a prophetic community distinct from the world. But only such an understanding can guide the church's life and mission.

Today, as in every age, the church struggles to be faithful to God in the political, social, and economic world. We must not equate Christian faith with any nation's way of life or with opposition to the ideologies of other nations. Nor can we afford to equate Christian faith with any economic or social system. Instead we must sense God's judgment on all political, social, and economic systems, including our own.

Still God does not call us out of the world; he rather sends us into the world. We therefore live as Christians when we discern what God is doing in the world and join God in his work. Worship should inspire and motivate us for such radical action.

Of course we will always risk disagreement and error when we try to say what God is doing and what we must do, but the church is called to live in that tension. To accomplish its mission the church is required to live in the world but not of it. That is not easy to do, of course. Every society asks of its religious institutions that they bless the way things are, and that is why those churches which support the status quo are often the most popular. Though they deny the Gospel, they fulfill the world's demand that they be communities of cultural continuity.

Christ calls his church, however, to be a community of change, to act with God in transforming the world into the community of our Lord and Savior Jesus Christ. To make an adequate response to that vocation is to live simultaneously in this world and in the community of God. We cannot escape from the world and be faithful. Neither can we become so enmeshed in the world that we lose our souls. To live on the boundary is difficult and demanding.

Nevertheless, the Scriptures remind us that we are a special people, a people with a peculiar memory—a memory of being continuously called to leave where we are and go somewhere else and be someone else, a people never staying put or holding on to present understandings and ways.

We are a people with a peculiar vision—a vision of a

world not yet realized and yet already come. In our worst moments we stop envisioning and believe it is well to celebrate and keep life as it is, but God haunts us by promising us a new age and pulling us toward its realization. Continuously, God demands that we be dissatisfied with life as it is. God judges us and provides us with a vision to inspire and stimulate us to action.

We are called to be a people with a peculiar hope—a hope that gives meaning to life as a pilgrim people on a mission under the power and purpose of the Gospel. It is a hope which proclaims that persons and institutions can change, that people and the public order can be transformed to more fully embody God's will for justice, harmony, liberation, community, and peace.

But what counts for us humans is not realizing this hope, but resisting evil. What matters is the human struggle against all that denies God's coming community and to that end we are called.

In our most recent memories there have been two quite different responses to God's call to Christian responsibility. The first was the liberal progressivism of the social Gospel, with its commitment to the gradual human transformation of society through human action. Following a disillusionment over the assumption of inevitable progress and human goodness came neo-orthodoxy with its focus on human sin and a shift from political and social change to an emphasis on the redemptive acts of God in history, on judgment and realism. Each possessed partial truth. Each was a corrective for the other. Neither alone was adequate. Both have been caricatured and criticized by advocates of the other and by those who shared neither of their understandings of the social dimensions of the Gospel.

Beginning and Ending with Faith

What is needed today is a new understanding that has no blind expectations of progress or belief in the capacity of human beings to build God's community. Founded upon a more radical understanding of God's action in history and a renewed social consciousness consistent with the biblical narrative, we need to work toward the equipping of persons and groups to engage in responsible action in society.

Along with the Christian faith through the ages we need to affirm that God is at work, especially in events and moments that liberate people from oppression and advance justice, peace, community, and well-being. God continues to reach out to those who suffer injustice, those who are excluded. Therefore, we believe that God sends us to work with others on behalf of God's coming community. We are charged to root out racism and prejudice from individuals and institutions, to correct the disparity between rich and poor nations, to stand with women and men of all races, ages, classes, and nationalities as they struggle for dignity, respect, power, and equity.

We know our efforts cannot bring in God's community, but faith plunges us into the struggle, and hope gives us courage and energy to live from reform to reform. God's new world and new humanity are surely coming, and we are called to live intelligently for that vision. Christian education must transmit this faith and hope. It must equip and stimulate us as individuals and churches to live for such ends. Only then can it truly claim the name Christian.

Ultimately the church exists for no other reason than to help make and keep human life genuinely human. That means that the church is to be that historic agency through which God overcomes the bondage to the institutions, power, and practices which have enslaved and oppressed persons and groups, enabling all persons to become the liberated, creative, visionary, historical actors as originally intended. It is, then, as a *witnessing community* that the church must be understood. The church has a story to tell, a vision to share, good news to proclaim. And that story, vision, and good news are communicated best through its life, its word-actions in the world. The structures and programs of the church can only be justified insofar as they enable the community of faith to be an historical agency through which God remakes the human world.

The church cannot afford to be an institution among institutions. It has a right to exist only as a body of disciplined believers committed to the historical mission of witnessing in word and deed to God's community-building.

The Christian church has no alternative but to engage in actions which challenge the evils of society—poverty, ignorance, disease, oppression, injustice, war, and prejudice—and to attempt to create more human alternatives. The Christian faith community therefore is called: to stop contributing to our social ills; to take a stand on social issues; to raise a prophetic voice against injustice; to take positive action on behalf of liberation; to influence public opinion; to join with others working for social justice; to identify with and become the advocate to the cause of the outsider; to eliminate the chasm between personal and social religion (why don't we turn the current enthusiasm for the Holy Spirit—long overdue—into a concern for the manifestation of the works of the Holy Spirit?); and to respond to people's hunger for spiritual life by relating worship and prayer to social action, for both together are the work (liturgy) of a faith community.

Some will say this is expecting too much of the church. But is that the issue? Perhaps the church has erred when it tried to make itself into a "perfect" community of "saints," but so did it err when it refused to set standards for its life and its members' lives. There is another possible position. The Christian community of faith can be clear on what it believes and what it is to be. Then, without ruling some people in and some out, or believing that it is always living the "perfect" life to which it is called, it can struggle continuously to live under the judgment and inspiration of the Gospel to the end that God's community comes and God's will is done. Only an educational paradigm that supports and encourages such an understanding of the church can be defended or advocated.

IMPLICATIONS

As a result of these theological musings, a few principles emerge that suggest directions for framing a new paradigm or model for religious education.

First, while maintaining a necessary particularity for education—deliberate, systematic, and sustained efforts— our new paradigm must broaden the context of Christian education to include every aspect of our individual and corporate lives within an intentional, covenanting, pilgrim, radical, counter-cultural, tradition-bearing faith community. A viable paradigm or model for religious education needs to focus upon the radical nature of a Christian community where the tradition is faithfully transmitted through ritual and life, where persons as actors—thinking, feeling, willing, corporate selves—are nurtured and converted to radical faith, and where they are prepared and motivated for individual and corporate action in society on behalf of God's coming community.

Second, while the context or place of Christian education is best understood as a community of faith, the means of Christian education is best understood as the actions between and among faithful persons in an environment that supports the expansion of faith and equips persons for radical life in the world as followers of Jesus Christ.

Therefore, *a community of faith-enculturation paradigm* is the name I have chosen for a new understanding of religious education. That may not be catchy or provide crystal-clear images, but it does suggest a direction for the future worth exploring, and it is to that task we turn next.

CHAPTER THREE

In Search of Community

. . . Faith is communicated by a community of believers
and the meaning of faith is developed by its members out of
their history, by their interaction with each other, and in
relation to the events that take place in their lives.

C. Ellis Nelson

M Y CONTENTION is that the context or place of
religious education needs to be changed from an emphasis
on schooling to a community of faith. No longer is it helpful
or wise to emphasize schools, teachers, pupils, curricula,
classrooms, equipment, and supplies. Instead we need to
focus our attention on the radical nature and character of
the church as a faith community.

Ultimately, of course, a faith community is a gift from
God, a mystery which we celebrate in the sacraments and
acknowledge through lives lived under the judgment and
inspiration of the Gospel. Nevertheless, a community of
faith does seem to have certain characteristics that are iden-

tifiable and that can be helpful in evaluating our lives as a faithful people of God.

In a significant community the people share a common memory or tradition, common understandings and ways of life, and common goals and purposes. If such a community is to exist, there needs to be unity in essentials; that is, in the community's understandings, values, and ways. Diversity with a corresponding charity can only be tolerated in nonessentials, such as commitments to particular political, economic, or social causes, or to particular actions or strategies for change. A community possesses a clear identity. Pluralism is only possible or healthy when persons have an identity and are open to others. A faith community must agree on what it believes. Only then can the struggle to interpret those beliefs serve constructive ends. Diversity in interpretation can be valuable, but only if there is agreement on a statement of faith and the authority to be used as a guide to interpretation. Often the church tolerates too great a diversity in essentials and hence has no clear identity. When that occurs faith can neither be sustained nor transmitted, and community dissolves into institutional togetherness. Faith can only be nurtured within a selfconscious intentional community of faith.

Second, a community of faith must be small enough to maintain meaningful, purposeful interactions among its members. A church of over three hundred members can too easily avoid those interactions essential to the maintenance, transmission, and expansion of faith. Of course, in one important sense, the community of faith is universal, uniting together faithful persons of all tongues and races, here and beyond. However, for this greater community to have reality and meaning, we need to interact within the intimacy of a closely knit community in which fellowship and care for each other can be experienced, and in which the struggles of faith and life can be shared. Larger units can serve important organizational needs, but if they are to be fully constructive, we need to maintain the life of smaller communities within them. Without this sense of intimate community, the church becomes simply another institution in the society—and that we cannot afford to permit.

Third, true community necessitates the presence and interaction of three generations. Too often the church either lacks the third generation or sets the generations apart. Remember that the third generation is the generation of memory, and without its presence the other two generations are locked into the existential present. While the first generation is potentially the generation of vision, it is not possible to have visions without a memory, and memory is supplied by the third generation. The second generation is the generation of the present. When it is combined with the generations of memory and vision, it functions to confront the community with reality, but left to itself and the present, life becomes intolerable and meaningless. Without interaction between and among the generations, each making its own unique contribution, Christian community is difficult to maintain.

Last, a true community unites all those roles and its understanding of status are important to corporate life. For the Christian this means that a true faith community must be composed of persons with diverse gifts—apostles, prophets, teachers. Yet how often has the church been willing to support prophets in its midst? However, when we avoid the pain and torment of a prophet's presence, a community of Christian faith eludes us. Also, when the Christian church is divided by race, social, or economic status, nationality or ethnic origin, true Christian community is once again outside our grasp. And, of course, if one sex is restricted to particular roles or denied equal status, there can be no Christian community.

If our children are to have faith, we need to make sure that the church becomes a significant community of faith. To meet this challenge we need to take seriously the characteristics of community and we need to examine, evaluate, plan, and develop educational programs around three aspects of corporate life: the rituals of the people; the experiences persons have within the community; and the actions members of the community perform, individually and corporately, in the world.

RITUAL

By their rites will you know them is more than mere rhetoric, for no aspect of corporate life is more important than its rituals. Worship, therefore, is at the center of the church's life; indeed, the word orthodoxy means "right praise"—as well as "right belief." Ritual or cultic life sustains and transmits the community's understandings and ways. Our liturgies express the hidden meanings of our experience in relationship to the world, to others, and to God.

In Search of Community

There is no community without cultic life. We humans are made for ritual and, in turn, our rituals make us. That is why our liturgies are so difficult to change. It will always be easier and more acceptable to preach a radical sermon than to change the order of worship, because the structures of our rituals provide us with the means to order and reorder life amidst the demands of daily existence and the vicissitudes of change. Rituals telescope our understandings and ways, give meaning to our lives, and provide us with purposes and goals for living. That explains why, when our understanding or ways of life change, we tend to stop participating in the old rituals that once inspired and sustained us. It also explains why, after casting aside old rituals, one of our first needs is to birth new ones. Changes in our understandings and ways result in changes in our rituals, and changes in our rituals produce significant changes in our lives. Every reform movement in the history of the church has involved liturgical reform; indeed, the most revolutionary events in Christian history have always affected the church's rituals. When the prophets sensed that the people had forsaken their faith, they attacked their rituals; and when the people were in despair over their faith, they called them to return to their rituals.

Liturgy needs to become a major aspect of Christian education, but before that will be possible the character and role of rites and rituals need to be properly understood. Rituals are first of all orderly, predictable, and stereotyped. In a day when some old rituals have lost their meaning and we are experimenting with new rituals, we often forget the importance of order and predictability, which explains in part why those who are secure in past understandings are troubled by these experiments. Only those who are searching for new understandings find experiments with worship meaningful, but even they long for a day when order is re-established. The church's educational ministry needs to assume responsibilities for helping the faith community to understand its ritual life, evaluate its present liturgies, explore necessary new expressions, and provide proper preparation for meaningful participation.

In addressing these responsibilities it is important to consider (1) those rituals which help us to sustain and transmit our understandings and ways, and (2) those rituals which make meaningful the crises or transitions in our lives. The first I call *rites of community*. In the Christian faith community such rituals are best exemplified by the Sunday liturgy when the community gathers to celebrate its faith. There is no more important community gathering than the Sunday liturgy which telescopes the understandings of life and the preferred ways of life of those who celebrate together. To cease worshiping is to lose faith. To transmit faith to the next generation is to include them as participants in all the community's rituals.

Characteristically, the Christian faith community has ordered its Sunday liturgy in particular ways—ways which attempt to express in structure and content the Christian faith and life. This structure has assumed many forms, each related in significant ways to history and culture, but one common expression has taken the shape of a drama which begins when the people of God gather in the name of the Lord to hear his word as contained in the Scriptures and to have that word brought into the present through preaching. The community responds to the hearing of God's word by reaffirming its historic faith. "We believe," they say, and thereby summarize the Christian faith story and establish their identity. Having affirmed its faith, the community turns naturally to a concern for God's world, expressing it in prayers of intercession. These prayers are followed by prayers of confession. Week after week the community hears God's word, affirms its faith, and prays for the world, but much of life remains unchanged. The faithful need to confess their sins of omission and commission and hear God's word of acceptance. Only then can they boldly strive once again to make a proper offering, a personal and corporate commitment to live in the world as those who have received the grace of God and who intend to take up their crosses and follow after Christ. Following the offering, as disciples of Jesus Christ, they bind themselves together in community by sharing with each other the kiss of peace and celebrating the victory party of the people of God. In the joyful sharing of this thanksgiving feast with Christ they gather the strength and courage to go forth into the world as his disciples, and to that end they are commissioned and blessed.

While numerous other liturgies are possible, it is important to remember that our understandings of the Christian faith are always revealed in our rituals. It is, therefore, essential that a faith community continuously judge its ritual life by the Gospel. A corresponding search for understanding and the evaluation and reordering of ritual life are also important aspects of Christian education. Another is to prepare persons to meaningfully participate in the community's rituals.

Consider the possible significance of using the hour before the Sunday liturgy as an opportunity for education. What if a congregation, all ages together, gathered before the morning liturgy? At this time they could welcome new persons, share fellowship together, learn about and minister to each other's needs—all of which are ways of enhancing community life. Second, the people could prepare for the morning ritual by learning hymns, responses, and other aspects of the liturgy, thereby making participation meaningful. Third, the liturgy could be enhanced if the lectionary (lessons from the Scriptures to be read and preached) was used to provide content for a series of diverse intergenerational educational experiences and discussions among all the worshipers—children, youth, and adults. By uniting learning and liturgy, Christian education could be enhanced; more important, our faith could be transmitted to our children.

The second type of ceremony, which aids us in making the transitions or changes in our lives meaningful, I call *life crisis rites*. These community rituals help us to understand and affirm the most significant moments in our lives. In terms of faith, our major life crisis rites are related to the pilgrimage of faith and its significant turning points: baptism, first communion, confirmation, ordination, and last rites. Other crisis rites—marriage, divorce, coming of age, going away to school, a new home, a move, a new job, a serious illness, retirement—can also speak to changes in our human condition in the light of Christian faith.

To understand life crisis rites properly it is helpful to realize that they each have three related phases: (1) a separation phase marked by a ceremonial withdrawal of persons from their previous status, role, or state in the community; (2) a transition phase which prepares persons, through ceremonial events, training, and often ordeals for their new status, role, or state in the community; and (3) a reentry phase which, by a ceremony, establishes persons in their new status, role, or state, and reincorporates them in the community. Considering these stages in life crisis rites, it should be obvious that education can play a role, and indeed has a particularly important role to play, during the second or transition phase.

Further, education in a faith community has a special responsibility for preparing persons to participate in its life crisis liturgies. New forms of prebaptismal education are needed, as well as preparation and follow-up education for first communion and confirmation. Both the proper age or stage in life for participation, (Is confirmation best celebrated with children, youth, or adults?) and the sequence or relationship between them (Should baptism, first communion, confirmation be spread out over time or united together? And in what order?) need to be understood as theological, liturgical, *and* educational issues.

My personal preference is: baptism for children at birth; first communion around first or second grade, a new "covenanting" ritual in early adolescence (to be described in chapter four); confirmation in late adolescence; ordination into Christian vocations (for all) in mid-adulthood (again see chapter four); and last rites at death. In any case, Christian education should be related to preparation for these rituals. For example, consider prebaptismal education. As soon as a couple are aware that they are to be parents (by birth or adoption) they might come before the congregation to announce that fact, be blessed, receive the prayers and support of the congregation and, most important, have godparents called forth from the congregation to help them prepare for the presence of their child. For the next several months the parents, godparents, relatives living nearby, and other children in the family might gather for a weekly supper, liturgy, and educational program to prepare spiritually for their new responsibilities and to explore how best to nurture their children in Christian faith. If the expected child should die before birth, a supportive community would exist; and if the child is born, the parents would be prepared for their child's baptism and have a supportive community to aid them in fulfilling their baptismal vows. Family life education in intergenerational groupings could then provide helpful education after baptism.

A great deal more can and ought to be said about liturgy and education, but for now let me simply express once again my contention that the liturgical and ritual aspects of life in the church need to become a major dimension of Christian education. Ritual must always be at the heart of Christian education, for in the community's liturgy, story and action merge; in worship we remember and we act in symbolic ways which bring our sacred tradition and our lives together, providing us with both meaning and motivation for daily existence. That is why, if our children are to have faith, they must worship with us.

EXPERIENCE

It is difficult to overestimate the importance of experience in the shaping of our lives. I became conscious of this fact a number of years ago when I was the member of a commission for the White House Conference on Children. The government had gathered together the most diverse group of persons with whom I had ever worked, a caricature of every type of person you can imagine: such as the young black radical from the northeast, the elderly white conservative housewife from the midwest, the middle-aged corporation executive from the south. On the first day we met, there was so much hatred and confusion I thought we would never be able to write a report, but for a year we traveled across the country and shared experiences. We witnessed American Indian children having their mouths washed out with soap for speaking their native tongue, and other atrocities and injustices. I was then asked to write a first draft of our report and was given the instructions to write something that would be approved by everyone. I was told we could not tolerate a minority report so I struggled with that problem and all the conservative and radical persons who were to sign it. The result was a report filled with qualifying statements and hedges, and when it was read at our final meeting, the elderly white conservative housewife stood up, red faced, and exclaimed in words she surely had never uttered before, "This report isn't *radical* enough." Others agreed. It was rewritten and, like most government reports, was considered extremist and irrelevant. What had happened? We were different people; our experiences had changed us!

Similarly, the experiences we have in a community of faith are important for answering the question: Will our children have faith? We need to bring our experiences and offer them to others in our church under the judgment and inspiration of the Gospel. To engage in such reforming activity is to engage in Christian education. This conviction goes back to my first experiences in a faith community with a youth group I directed many years ago. Those were the days of large youth groups and some 298 young people were gathered in a large fellowship hall, while in the kitchen two boys were making popcorn. I began to hear shouting. "You are *not* going to put salt in the popcorn!" "I am *so* going to put salt in the popcorn!" Their voices got louder and then a body came through a wooden door. He had put salt in the popcorn! In the midst of the confusion the two boys disappeared and I was left with 298 youths wanting to know what we were going to do about them. At the time I didn't know what to do, so I said, "Let's sit down and talk about it." It was finally decided that the group would pay for the door, and the two boys would be invited back next week—to make popcorn in *two* bowls. A few days later I was in a discussion with Paul Tillich, and he said that the heart of the Gospel was being "accepted though unacceptable." That was a significant moment in my life because experience and the words of the Gospel were united.

Another transforming experience is also very clear in my memory. A few details have been changed to protect those involved. It occurred a short time ago as I was leading a youth-adult retreat. Four hundred of us, two hundred young people and two hundred adults, had gathered to explore our faith. By evening of the first day it was discovered that over $200 was missing from people's wallets. The boys and girls were separated; hostility and anger filled the air; there were accusations and despair. After two hours I called the group together and did the only thing I knew to do; I read the incident in the temple from the Gospel According to St. John. It is the story of a woman detected in adultery (John 7:53–58). The religious leaders wanted Jesus to condemn her, but he only said, "Let the one who is faultless throw the first stone." When no one did, he said to the woman: "Has no one condemned you?" "No one, sir," she said. Jesus replied, "No more do I. You may go. Do not sin again."

After that, I prayed for God's grace among us. At the end of the prayer, the young man who had stolen the money came forward to make his confession and return the money. They were going to send him home when someone cried, "Do you want to stay?" "Yes," he mumbled. "Stay! Stay!" everyone cried. "Let us sing 'Amazing Grace'," I exclaimed, and we did. With tears running down their faces, one person after another came forward to embrace the boy.

We sometimes get so concerned about telling people things that we forget the tremendous significance of experience. I can recall another gathering at the home of the theologian Paul Tillich during my years at divinity school. We were sharing the struggles of our souls, our doubts and despair, and I suppose we expected the great theologian to say something. Instead he went to his record player and turned on the "Credo" from Bach's "B Minor Mass." The response Tillich made to our struggles with faith was to offer us the experience of listening to the historic community of faith affirm its faith in song.

Persons learn first enactively through their experience, then by imaging (stories), and last of all through the use of signs (conceptual language). For faith, it is therefore especially important to acknowledge that the most significant and fundamental form of learning is experience. Later a person may "image" that experience, and even later conceptualize it. But we begin by experiencing life in a community which seeks the good of others, then we learn the story of the Good Samaritan, and finally through reflection on our experience ("doing theology") we symbolically conceptualize the community of God in terms of love, justice, and equity. Each of these steps in learning occurs in order, and each is essential to the following step. But at the beginning is experience.

A community of faith needs to be concerned about the character and nature of the experiences persons share in community. Using the community of faith as the context for Christian education encourages us to evaluate our actions and interactions in the light of the Gospel, even as we strive together to frame the sort of community life that witnesses to the action of God in our lives. We must always remember: If our children are to have Christian faith, the life they experience in the church must be a distinctive expression of the church faith story.

ACTION

Remember that it was the life of Christians in the world that converted persons to Christian faith. Too often we forget that our individual and corporate actions in society are the true test of our faith. Just as we are more apt to *act* our way into new ways of thinking than *think* our way into new ways of acting, we are more apt to learn the implications of faith through the ways we are encouraged and stimulated to act in the world than through our study of Christian ethics. Our vocation as Christians is in the world, and as children of God we are called to join God in his liberating historic actions. God is at work in the world on behalf of peace, justice, and love. To know God is to join in his history-making, and thus we need both to explore the nature and character of our individual and corporate actions in the world as aspects of our faith community's life and to make these actions a significant part of our educational ministry.

When we act under the judgment and inspiration of the Gospel to the end that God's community comes and God's will is done, we become a community of Christian faith. If our children are to have faith, our educational ministry must prepare us and stimulate us to engage in Christian actions.

As a Christian faith community we engage in personal, interpersonal, and social actions. For example, most people agree that if there are people in the community who are poor, in need of food, shelter, or care, we as Christians should respond. Indeed, through the years, personal service to those in need has exemplified the church's concern for others. Sometimes, of course, our giving of Thanksgiving baskets and Christmas presents has been patronizing and self-aggrandizing, but they were meant as acts of mercy and are to be affirmed as acts of Christian love. Nevertheless, to depend on personal actions is inadequate because of the staggering numbers in need. Interpersonal forms of action which we support, but which are conducted by professionals, are also necessary. A good example is found in our national welfare system and food stamp program. Since these methods have often been inadequate or oppressive, the church needs to take the lead in seeing that such attempts to meet need within our present economic system are developed, supported, and reformed to truly benefit the needy.

Ultimately, however, even such interpersonal actions are inadequate to achieve economic justice and meet the needs of the poor. Social action is also, therefore, incumbent upon the church and this includes engaging in political activity to reform our economic system until justice and equity are achieved. For example, the church might take a stand on behalf of democratic socialism, and support the establishment of a guaranteed minimum income for all people and a maximum income above which no one has a right to acquire money or property. While such specific social actions may not be easily agreed upon (there is no specifically Christian economic system), I contend that the church, if it is to be a community of faith, is called by the radical nature of the Gospel to consider just such radical social actions and continuously struggle against all evil.

The church is called by God, not to be a community of cultural continuity in support of the status quo but a countercultural community of social change. Only if we come to understand our life as a faith community in terms of our actions in the world; only if we evaluate the nature and character of our personal, interpersonal, and social actions; only if we motivate and enable the church to be a community of cultural change acting on behalf of the Gospel; only then will we be a faith community worthy of Christ's name.

It may be exceedingly difficult to get a local church or denomination to agree on a plan for action, but I believe that it is essential for the church to act politically. The doctrine of the separation of church and state was created to free the church from control by the state and to secure the right of the church to judge and influence the state. To deny or ignore these rights and responsibilities is to misunderstand and be unfaithful to the church's mission. No one ever said that this would be easy, but a proper and adequate educational ministry should equip, motivate, and aid the church in fulfilling its corporate mission in the world.

However, one warning! Too often the church, acting on its emotions and sense of good will, has been mindless; the results have been disastrous. There is no alternative for serious study and intellectual investigation. Too often religious education has neglected its responsibility to aid the community in securing the facts, investigating alternative actions and their consequences, and designing political strategies. Social action without knowledge and hard-nosed thinking is irresponsible. The church needs to train its people to *think* politically, socially, economically, theologically, and ethically. Religious education cannot place those needs too high on its list of priorities.

Still, as it reflects on action as an aspect of its educational ministry, the church has yet another related responsibility. Each of us spends our daily life engaged in some activity; we need help in turning jobs into vocations, and our daily decisions into ethical decisions informed by Christian faith. Christian education needs to address such needs.

Finally, an important word: We face no greater evil in society than racism, to which every institution, the church included, continues to contribute. The educational ministry of the church must help us to understand how we participate in this injustice and then equip and motivate us to effect change in the institutions of which we are a part. Now as always the church is challenged to tell its story to the world by what it stands for and what it does. Our educational ministry must assist us in doing just that. Our children will have faith, only if we do.

Will Our Children Have Faith?

Historically, all education has vacillated between three concerns: knowledge, persons, and society. Consider for a moment how we train leaders for the church's ministry. Divinity schools or seminaries have sometimes emphasized one or another of these three foci in their curriculum. When a concern for "knowledge" has dominated, they have focused on either a core of knowledge and/or the disciples of biblical studies, church history, theology, and ethics. When a concern for "persons" has dominated, they have focused on the spiritual development and faith of their students. And when a concern for "society" has dominated, they have focused on the vocation of ministry and such specific skills as preaching, counseling or administration (rarely education).

While most seminaries include all three foci in their curriculum rhetoric, one or another has usually assumed greater worth. For example, while a core of knowledge once dominated our seminary curricula, the trend now is moving to skills for ministry. A similar analysis can be made of education in the church. However, it is most important to affirm that all three are equally essential for Christian education. We can not afford to let one or another dominate or be ignored. Our rituals, our experiences in the church, and our individual and corporate actions in the world need to be judged and inspired by (1) how well they are informed by and express our Christian tradition, (2) how well they enhance and sustain our spiritual lives, and (3) how well they equip and motivate us for action in the world. If our children are to have faith, Christian education must be whole. That means making sure that a Christian understanding of the tradition, persons, and society influences and is expressed in the community's rituals, experiences, and actions in the world.

THE TRADITION

A community of faith is essentially a community interacting with a living tradition. The tradition we bear as a faith community is essentially and primarily a story, a story of God's mighty deeds and actions in history. The Christian story is a story about a vision. In the beginning God has a vision of a world at one with itself, a world of peace, justice, freedom, equity, whole community, and the well-being of all. It is the world God intends.

God creates persons in his image, historic actors who he intends will live in and for his vision. But God also grants persons the freedom to say yes or no to his vision. And so the plot thickens. We humans are more interested in our visions than God's vision. We create systems ("principalities and powers") which benefit some of us but not all of us. As a result of our own selfish actions we become isolated from nature, ourselves, each other, and God.

But God persists in seeking after us. God calls a community into being to witness to his vision. And he takes the side of those who are either kept outside or oppressed by the systems we humans create. God, biased toward the hurt and the have-nots, acts on their behalf that his vision might be realized. God liberated the slaves in Egypt, patiently pulled them toward his vision, and established a covenant with them to live as his visionary community.

Will Our Children Have Faith?

Still, it doesn't work, for as soon as we humans begin to receive the blessings of God's vision we act to keep those blessings for ourselves alone. God continues to raise up prophets to remind us of his intentions for his world, and a faithful remnant keeps the story of God's vision alive.

Nevertheless, it is as if we are in bondage to the social forces, to the political, economic, and social systems we have built. Over and over again some individuals catch a glimpse of God's vision and commit their lives to its realization; yet that vision still remains a lost dream. So God makes a decision and God acts again, enters our human condition, becomes incarnate in Jesus of Nazareth—the storyteller, doer of deeds, healer of hurts, advocate of the outsider, liberator of the oppressed. Through Jesus the good news is announced: God's community has come. In the absurdity and foolishness of the cross, God acts to liberate us from bondage to the principalities and powers. Nothing—no social, political, or economic power—can hold us any longer. So, on Easter morning the disciples behold the dawn of God's coming community. Love using power has overcome oppression.

Yet the dawn of hope is not yet the high noon of God's community come on earth. Darkness still covers much of the land, people are still oppressed, wars continue, poverty and hunger prevail, injustice is perpetuated, and the mass of humanity is still marginal to God's promise. Many of us who claim the name Christian continue to frustrate God's vision and live as if we do not understand the implications of the Gospel. We bless our individualism and competition, we say this is the best of all possible worlds, we justify our way of life.

God calls prophets forth to remind us of his vision and

the radical demands it places on our lives. The Gospel itself judges and inspires us. Here and there some live according to God's will and for God's coming community. Each week the community of faith gathers to celebrate its hope, to point to the signs of God's coming community, to announce that we are liberated from the principalities and powers, and to stimulate us to act with God for his vision.

The church is the bearer of that story. And when that story becomes our story we will know what the name Christian means. Education is concerned that the story be known and owned; it is concerned that this story be understood and applied. We had better agree on the story, for it needs to inform everything we do and say, and it needs to be expressed in our individual and corporate lives. It is a story that needs to be told and made incarnate in the life of a faith community. But that presents us with a difficulty, for we have all too often been willing to turn the story into dogmas and doctrines that lack charisma and power. Worse than that, we have continued either to tell only preferred parts of the story or to misinterpret the story when it doesn't benefit us, turning the Gospel into an opiate of personal piety and ignoring its call to social liberation.

We too easily forget that the message of the prophet Isaiah is delivered to a community, a people, and not an individual or one particular group. We ignore the fact that his message is a message to a people who have been in bondage and oppression, waiting for a redemptive act of God. To the have-nots, the oppressed, repressed, depressed, and suppressed peoples of the world, God speaks in the prophet Isaiah a word of comfort (Isaiah 40). In our sin we misunderstand that message and do not hear its word of judgment on the rest of us. Of course, it is a message of judgment tempered by mercy, but mercy which requires repentance and a changed life. God is putting things right in his world, bringing to fruition his visionary community, and we are called to join God in his revolutionary historic social activity. That is the story we have to tell; that is the story that needs to judge and inspire every aspect of our life. How we interpret and apply that story is also important. It would be well for us to realize that the Bible is "poetry plus" and not "science minus." For too long we have permitted and encouraged only one limited means of interpretation.

Two and a half centuries ago there was a struggle within the faculty at St. Thomas School in Leipzig between the cantor of the school, J. S. Bach, and the new rector, J. A. Ernesti, a pioneer in the literary historical criticism of the Bible. Bach believed that the Scriptures could best be understood and interpreted through the use of music and worship, while Ernesti believed that reason dictated a more scholarly approach to biblical interpretation. Today we desperately need to remind ourselves that *both* the artistic and the rationalistic perspectives have value, and that a return to congregational singing of the St. Matthew Passion is as important for understanding and interpreting the story of our faith as the critical literary-historical study of its message. In any case the tradition must judge, inform, and inspire every aspect of our lives, and Christian education must see that we come to know, understand, interpret, live, and act that tradition if our children are to have faith.

In Search of Community

There are days when it appears as if some professional educators believe that human beings are only minds. Mirroring the current emphasis in psychology and pedagogy, Christian educators have tended to emphasize cognition and thinking. We have, it seems, turned faith into a way of knowing and nothing else. Of course knowing is important and thinking is important; in light of the anti-intellectualism that has infected so much of church life, that cannot be overemphasized. Nevertheless, thinking is not sufficient in and of itself. I would like to defend the point that we are essentially agents, historic actors whose lives are best understood as a gestalt of thinking, feeling, and willing. We are created to act in the world as spiritual beings and that is why we are called to live lives of prayer—the spiritual life—through continual adoration, confession, petition, intercession, and thanksgiving.

Adoration, as I understand it, is focusing our lives upon God. It is the life of the dreamer and visionary that makes it possible to view every aspect of life as a miracle. *Confession* is the continual self-examination of our personal and social lives in the presence of God; it is living under the judgment of God's will. *Petition and intercession* are bringing our desires for self and others in line with God's desires or attuning our hearts and minds and wills to that of God. *Thanksgiving* is our active daily expression of gratitude to God for his continuing action in history, a celebrative awareness of God's actions in our midst.

We are told by Jesus to pray without ceasing, but surely that does not mean to live on our knees uttering words to God. Rather, prayer is living consciously in the presence of a God who acts in history through persons and communities to establish his community of love, power, and justice. Prayer involves living with a conscious awareness of God's presence, of uniting our wills with God's in common reflective action. Prayer is a radical ethical activity, a passionate action that results from both intuitive and intellectual activity.

Two modes of consciousness are possible for human beings. One is intellectual and focuses on the universal and the abstract, and is characterized by verbal, linear, conceptual, and analytical activities. The other is intuitional and focuses on the syncretic and the experiential, and is characterized by nonverbal, creative, nonlinear, relational activities. The development and integration of both modes of consciousness is essential to the spiritual life.

Numerous examples of the spiritual life in the Bible support such an understanding. Operating from that perspective, the prophets (understanding history as the place of God's creativity) used their intuitive powers to hear the voice of God, and their intellects to reflect on God's word so they might act with God in history.

Moses' intuitive experience with the burning bush led him to reflect on his life and bring to his people a vision and message of liberation. The intuitive awareness of Christ's presence in the breaking of the bread at Emmaus led the disciples to lives of radical apostleship. None of these experiences or their resulting acts were purely rational or intuitional. Each represents a worldly intuitive experience which, through the use of the intellect, led to new sorts of moral behavior.

To understand persons as thinking, feeling, and willing historical actors is to support the growth and development of a person's intellectual and intuitive skills as well as his or her historical awareness. Christian education requires that we help persons regain their God-given ability to wonder and create; to dream and fantasize, imagine and envision; to sing, paint, dance, and act. It requires a recovery of our natural ability for ecstasy; our appreciation of the new, the marvelous, the mysterious; and a sensual and kinesthetic awareness. It requires a recovery of our God-given talent to express ourselves emotionally and nonverbally.

Concern for the religious affections must once again become a central concern of church education, and participation in the arts must become an essential focus of our educational ministries. We need also to focus on the development of historical awareness, and that will not be easy. We live in a historical time because we have been taught our history as a meaningless collection of dates, names, and places. Few of us are conscious of a meaningful past, and most of us consider the past we do recall as irrelevant to the present. As a result we are trapped in the present. Storytelling needs to become a natural and central part of church life, and we must learn to tell God's story as *our* story. No longer can we explain how some Israelites were once in bondage in Egypt and God saved them. (Who cares?) Instead we need to explain how *we* were once oppressed in Egypt and how God liberated *us*. We must again become a history-bearing community of faith and a storytelling people who seek to communicate God's story as our story. We need to remember that as persons we are actors in history; indeed faith is action and our faith is best revealed in our actions. If our children are to have faith, every aspect of church life must be inspired, judged, and informed by how well it nurtures our spiritual lives as thinking, feeling, willing people of God who act individually and corporately in the world to reveal the Gospel.

Church education has most often vacillated between a concern for persons and a concern for the tradition. We typically forget that we are corporate selves called to live in but not of the world. The community of faith has a vocation as a countercultural community and not as a mirror of the society, for it is called to give witness through word and deed to an alternative to life as it is.

In order for us to take our vocation in the world seriously, we need visions, hope, and power. And we need to ask to what extent our rituals, our experiences in the community of faith, and our action in the world express God's vision for humanity. Our society, the church included, is largely without visions, which means without clear and adequate goals. And thus the question—Will our children have faith?—is especially pertinent. Without visions the people perish, but God has given us a vision expressed by the Hebrew word *Shalom* and in the metaphor of the kingdom—or better, the community—of God: It is life in the world characterized by well-being, peace, liberation, justice, and whole community. The people of God are called to live for this vision and the church's educational ministry is given the responsibility of transmitting and sustaining that vision and enhancing its understanding.

Of course it is not enough to have visions; we need to have hope of their realizations. Christian hope boldly and confidently affirms that despite all evidence to the contrary, God's community has come, is coming, and will come in all its glory. To live and die for that vision makes sense and is worth any price. To live in the hope of the Gospel is to search for where God is acting in the word and join God in his activity. Hope founded in Christ has no alternative but to engage in social action that challenges the evils of society and creates more human alternatives. Of course only God will establish God's community in God's good time, but we are called to act faithfully, to struggle against all evil, and to live in hope. That may mean moving from one human reform to another, always judging the inadequacies of our last reform and striving for a better alternative. Christian education needs to help us live in and for that hope which inspires the continual struggle for justice and equity no matter what the odds or disappointments.

In addition to visions and hope we also need power—the wisdom, skills, know-how, and motivation—to act politically, socially, and economically in the world. Christian education needs to have as a primary responsibility the equipment and motivation of the people of God for corporate action in the world. We must never forget that our Christian vocation is in the world and that Christian educators must be engaged in helping us acquire the skills necessary to be responsible political and social agents. No aspects of our educational ministry have been more neglected. One of the greatest challenges facing Christian education is in enabling the church to be a witnessing community of faith. Only if we see that task as equally as important as our concern for the tradition and the spiritual lives of persons will our educational ministry fulfill its vocation and our children have faith.

Will Our Children Have Faith?

Using the radical nature and character of a faith community as the context or place for Christian education means using every aspect of our church's life for education—our rituals and preparation for participation, the experiences we have and provide within the community of faith, and the individual and corporate actions we inspire and equip persons to engage in. It means examining and judging our total life as a community of faith to see how well we live and transmit our Christian story or tradition, how well we minister to the total needs of whole persons in community, and how well we prepare and motivate individuals and communities to act on behalf of God's coming community in the world. This means understanding religious education in terms of a continuing struggle to reform the church.

If we make our life in a community of faith the context of Christian education, it will mean living each day under the judgment and inspiration of the Gospel to the end that God's community comes and God's will is done. The willingness to affirm and accept this understanding is the challenge of Christian education today; it is also the basis for an answer to the question: Will our children have faith?

CHAPTER FOUR

Life Together

> The central question is: How can the community educate for true and living faith and not merely for conformity to the accepted norms of belief and conduct within the nurturing fellowship?
>
> *Philip H. Phenix*

IN RESPONSE to the question asked by this book, it is easier to name the context for Christian education than it is to name the means. Instruction—teaching and learning—is not sufficient. But what are the alternatives? In *Generation To Generation* I introduced the concept "intentional socialization." I still believe it is a helpful concept, but as a result of theological reflections I have become increasingly wary of its use. Intentional socialization implies that someone does something to someone else. While the concept wisely broadens the context of Christian education to include every aspect of life in the church and makes us more mindful of our "hidden curriculum," it still gives the impression that we can and ought to be concerned about determining the life and faith of another. That, I want to question!

Perhaps it would be better to begin with the question:

Will Our Children Have Faith?

What does it mean to be Christian together? Such a question turns our attention from behavioral objectives for others to the character and quality of life lived together in a community of faith. Christian faith implies the need to focus on the mutuality of our engagements with each other, thereby eliminating all categories such as teacher and student, adult (the one who knows) and child (the one who needs to know), socializer and socializee. For these reasons, I have chosen the word "enculturation" to characterize educational method in a faith community.

While much socialization literature has a tendency to emphasize how the environment, experiences, and actions of others influence us, enculturation emphasizes the process of interaction between and among persons of all ages. It focuses on the interactive experiences and environments within which persons act to acquire, sustain, change, and transmit their understandings and ways. In enculturation one person is not understood as the actor and another the acted upon, but rather both act, both initiate action, and both react. It is the nature, character, and quality of these interactive experiences among people of all ages within a community of faith that best describes the means of Christian education.

While most instructional literature has a tendency to emphasize imparting knowledge or skill to another person or the deliberate attempt to produce specific desired learning outcomes in another, enculturation emphasizes what one person has to bring to another and the dialogical relationship between equals.

The language of instruction does not encourage us to think in terms of interaction. Therefore, some people act as if all essential knowledge and human possibility are within us at birth. They choose to remove themselves and as many other barriers to maturation as possible in order to encourage a person's natural growth to fulfillment. Others act as if a person at birth is an empty vessel which is to be filled, and they, therefore, must assume responsibility for what that person should be and know. Of course these are exaggerations, but they do explain and describe, even if in extreme terms, the varied assumptions and behavior of some educators.

Neither view, in my opinion, is adequate from either a theological or pedagogical perspective. In one important sense, each of us has faith at birth; it is not, therefore, given to us by others. Still our faith requires that we interact with other faithing selves to actualize itself and to develop its character and content. To understand faith and its content we need to focus our attention on the experiences of interaction between and among faithing persons in a self-conscious tradition bearing community of faith. What is important is not what we strive to give to another, but what we share and the various ways we strive to be Christian together within a community of faith.

In the 50s and 60s a few religious educators affirmed a similar position. They spoke of the language of relationships, dialogical education, and experiential learning. They spoke of life together in community. But the schooling-instructional paradigm prevented their position from receiving a fair hearing.

Of course, the idea was not new to them. Much earlier, John Dewey had defended a developmental-interactional view of education which stressed the importance of experiences that foster interaction between persons and their environment. Indeed, anthropologists interested in learning have always spoken of interactions between persons and their communities. And even the teachers of the early Sunday school movement shared similar convictions.

In 1905 John Vincent, the great Methodist leader of the Sunday school movement, then in his later years, gave an address at the Eleventh International Sunday School Convention in Toronto, Canada. It was entitled "A Forward Look for the Sunday School," and he began with an important observation, namely, that it is possible to make too much of method, of recent educational theory, of curricula, teaching, and intellectual training. He explained that the Sunday school, in its desire to gratify modern education, was in danger of making a blunder and of sacrificing good things that are old. Then Vincent made a prediction: In the future the Sunday school will be less like a school and more like a home. Its program will focus on conversation and the interaction of people rather than the academic study of the Bible or theology. The Sunday school will be a place where friends deeply concerned about Christian faith will gather to share life together.

In 1816 J. A. James wrote *The Sunday School Teacher's Guide*. He opened with the conviction that teaching religion is something more than giving instruction. He further explained that the accumulation of biblical facts and figures and the memorization of passages of Scripture are an insignificant part of religious education, and that teaching is not to be an end in itself but a means to an end. James went on to describe the Sunday schools he knew best, first telling of children, youth, and adults preparing for and celebrating special occasions, such as Christmas, Easter, Thanksgiving, Missionary Day, and Decision Day. In a chapter entitled "We Learn By Doing," he described life in the Sunday school and included plays and musicals, games, hikes and hunts, parties and picnics, social service projects and community activities in which children, youth, parents, and grandparents participated together. The function of the Sunday school, with its variety of programs, was to give persons an opportunity to share life with other faithful selves, to experience the faith in community, to learn the Christian story and to engage in Christian actions. The key to these Sunday schools was not curriculum, teaching, learning strategies, or organization; it was people in community.

Benjamin Jacob, the Baptist layman who helped to transform the Sunday school into a worldwide movement, spoke of teaching as leading others by example on the road to spiritual maturity. Children, he pointed out, may or may not study their Bibles as diligently as desired, but they will study the lives of the adults they meet in the church. And so teachers must be models of what they desire others to become; they are to be spiritual mentors and not instructors.

In 1887 John Vincent wrote *The Modern Sunday School,* in which he described the Sunday school as a modern title for an ancient and apostolic service of the church. It is, he explained, a school first and foremost for disciples and it is a place where persons share their faith with each other. Vincent presented a variety of roles a teacher might play: he can entertain his pupils and keep them happy; he can work at winning their admiration; he can make them into good scholars who know the Bible and the church's doctrines. Vincent accepted none of these. Instead, he listed the spiritual qualities needed by teachers so that they may share their faith and thus aid in the spiritual growth and development of those they meet. A number of years later Senabaugh contended in *The Small Church School* that not just anyone can teach, for religion is caught more than taught and we cannot teach what we do not know and believe. Religion, he said, is an experience, and we cannot communicate anything that we have not verified. The teacher may teach about Christianity, but if he is to communicate Christ he must live in fellowship with him.

The old Sunday school appears to have cared most about creating an environment where people could be Christian together and where persons could experience Christian faith and see it witnessed to in the lives of significant people. The old Sunday school seemed to be aware of the importance of the affections, of storytelling, of experience, of community sharing, and of role models. While many of these concerns remain in the rhetoric of the modern church school movement, we seem to have created an institution more concerned with teaching strategies, instructional gimmicks, and curricular resources than with spiritual mentors; more concerned with age-graded classes for cognitive growth than with communities concerned with the affections; more concerned with the goals of knowing about the Bible, theology, and church history than with communities sharing, experiencing, and acting together in faith.

Verbal language, both spoken and written, has dominated Christian education for too long. Perhaps as far as Christian faith is concerned, we have attached too literal an interpretation to the primacy of the word. By sanctifying the oral and verbal traditions, we have lost something of the richness of the early church where the great truths of the community were enshrined in shared experience.

At the turn of the century, W. G. E. Cunnyngham wrote *Sunday School*. His main point was this: If one does not believe a person, one will not believe what that person says. Children, he continued, are close observers of character. They deal with the concrete and not the abstract; with them, actions speak louder than words.

The challenge facing the church is in the bland, unconverted, ignorant lives of its members. Until adults in the church are knowledgeable in their faith, have experienced the transforming power of the Gospel, live radical lives characteristic of the disciples of Jesus Christ, no new curriculum, no new insights on learning, no new teacher-training programs, and no new educational technology will save us.

Remember the parables of Jesus about the hidden treasure and the pearl of great price? The question we need to ask is this: Do I have in my experience anything to offer for which anyone would conceivably want to sell all they have to obtain? The quality of our faith will always reveal what we *are*. And what we *are* will in the end determine the value and effect of what we do. We must, therefore, pay attention first of all to ourselves.

The language of instruction can too easily lead us astray. It encourages us to be concerned for what we want our pupils to be or become. When we think "instruction," we focus our attention on what we want someone else to know, what we want someone else to feel, or how we want someone else to behave. We establish learning objectives for others, while parents legitimately ask us when we are going to teach their child about the Bible or what Christians believe or what is right and wrong.

But subject matter is not the issue; object matter is! As Albert Camus once said, if a thought is to change the world, it must first change the life of the person who carries it; it must become an example. The important questions are simply, but profoundly: What do I have to bring to another? What is truly mine that I have to share with others?

The most important questions a person can ask are: How can I be what I say I am? How can I live what I profess? There ought to be some identifiable difference between the person who claims the name of Christ and someone who denies him. If we truly are in Christ there should be qualities, characteristics, dispositions, and understandings discernible in our inner and outward lives.

There is no shadow of doubt in the New Testament that a professed Christian should be able to be known as such. Christian faith, says St. Paul in his letter to the Galatians (5:13–26), involves a fundamental change at the core of our being, a change brought about by the nature of our relationship to Christ and by the inner presence of the Holy Spirit. Nobody can rejoice in Christ and then go and do just as they please. There is a life appropriate to our calling. There are fruits of the spirit that are indicators of Christian faith.

The Christian faith invites women and men to a new level of existence, and the Gospel announces that this radically different sort of life is possible. But if we who proclaim the Gospel do not live it, then what? The answer to this question explains why enculturation—the interactions in community between faithful persons—is more adequate than instruction for understanding educational method in a faith community. Namely because the process of enculturation encourages us to consider our own faith and life with others. Instruction tends to encourage us to focus on the faith and life of the other, and therefore avoids the issue of how faith is sustained and transmitted.

A current issue facing Christian ethics may provide an interesting set of insights for understanding what is at stake in the choice between instruction and enculturation. It can be stated in this way: At a time when medical knowledge enables doctors to save and sustain life as never before, the value of doing so is increasingly questioned. What should we do with hopeless cases of people not imminently dying but so ill or handicapped or distraught as to face meaningless lives that are not worth living?

There are two alternative ways of viewing this problem: One can be described as the "quality-of-life" view and the other the "equality-of-life" view. The first encourages us to base our decisions to maintain life on utilitarian grounds such as social worth, to equate human dignity with control, to believe that to be dependent is to be less than human, and to maintain that certain forms of life are not human. The second asserts that life is a basic right of all, a right not to be qualified by another's assessment of the quality of any individual's life. Life itself confers dignity; life itself has worth. The living are equal in that each has worth as a human being. Life itself has value, and intentionally destroying it is morally wrong. This position maintains that the only question to be raised is whether or not we are indeed loving God and loving our neighbor. The moral question is not whether or not the other is a person, but whether we are the kinds of persons who will care for them without doubting their worth.

My personal conviction is that the second position is Christian. And I contend that a similar issue faces us when we decide on a method for Christian education. Under the rubrics of teaching and learning, or socialization, we have tended to emphasize our responsibility for deciding what another should know, be, and do. We want to know how we can make others into Christians, how we can put information about Christianity into their heads, how we can provide others with Christian experience, or how we can modify others behavior until they act as we believe Christians should act.

We need a new way of thinking about educational method, a way that emphasizes what *we* know, what *we* are and what *we* do. It is a way that forces us to focus on ourselves and not on the other. We cannot, as Christians, busy ourselves with deciding on the quality of another's life. We need to affirm the equality of all lives, and when we do, we shall begin to have an alternative understanding of educational method. Christian education needs to affirm the value of each life as equal before God. Our responsibility is to make our own life consistent with our calling and to share that life with others. We need to acknowledge not only the worth of others, but our need of their life and witness for our own growth in faith.

Shared experience, story telling, celebration, action, and reflection between and among equal "faithing" selves within a community of faith best helps us understand how faith is transmitted, expanded, and sustained. And so I contend that understanding the processes of *interaction* in community between "faithing" selves—what I have called enculturation—is the best way to understand educational method in a faith community.

Life Together

FAITH AND ITS EXPANSION

Faith, as I have used the word, is a verb. Faith is a way of behaving which involves knowing, being, and willing. The content of faith is best described in terms of our world-view and value system, but faith itself is something we do. Faith is an action. It results from our actions with others, it changes and expands through our actions with others, and it expresses itself daily in our actions with others.

After reflection on my own and other's faith pilgrimages, I have been able to describe four distinctive styles of faith. This conceptualization is not original, and I was first influenced to think about a stage theory for the development of faith through the important research of my friend James Fowler. Since we began communicating, however, I have proceeded in directions for which only I can be held responsible. Nevertheless, I do need and want to acknowledge my early debt, and to suggest that Fowler's research may necessitate significant changes in my own ideas.

At this point, I am prepared to suggest that faith (understood as a way of behaving) can, if provided with the proper interactive experiences, expand through four distinctive *styles* of faith. Each style of faith to be described is a generalization, and none are meant to be boxes into which persons are placed; neither are they to be used as judgments upon ourselves or others. I have named the first style of faith, *experienced faith;* the second, *affiliative faith;* the third, *searching faith;* and the fourth, *owned faith*. I have tried many ways to describe the relationship between these styles of faith and the best I've found, though still inadequate, is drawn from the analogy of a tree.

First, a tree with one ring is as much a tree as a tree with four rings. A tree in its first year is a complete and whole tree, and a tree with three rings is not a better tree but only an expanded tree. In a similar way, one style of faith is not a better or greater faith than another. Experienced faith, the first identifiable style, is complete and whole faith. One seeks to act with other faithing selves in community and hence to expand into new styles of faith, not so as to possess better or greater faith, but only to fulfill one's faith potential.

Second, a tree grows if the proper environment is provided, and if such an environment is lacking, the tree becomes arrested in its expansion until the proper environment exists. Each tree, however, does its own "growing" and has its own unique characteristics. Similarly, we expand from one style of faith to another only if the proper environment, experiences, and interactions are present; and if they are not, then our expansion of faith is arrested. Of course no style of faith is natural to any particular age and everyone can expand into a new style providing the proper interactions with other faithing souls is present.

Third, a tree acquires one ring at a time in a slow and gradual manner. We do not see that expansion, although we do see the results, and surely we are aware that you cannot skip rings, moving from a one-ring to a three-ring tree. The same is true of faith. We expand from one style of faith to another slowly and gradually (it cannot be rushed), adding one style at a time in an orderly process over time.

Fourth, as a tree grows, it does not eliminate rings but adds each ring to the ones before, always maintaining all the previous rings as it expands. It is the same with faith. As we expand in faith we do not leave one style of faith behind to acquire a new style but, on the contrary, each new style is added to the previous ones. We do not outgrow a style of faith and its needs but expand it by adding new elements and new needs. Indeed, if the needs of an earlier style of faith cease to be met, persons have a tendency to return to that earlier style of faith. Once, however, these needs are again satisfied persons return to their farthest expanded style of faith.

Faith is an action which includes thinking, feeling, and willing and it is transmitted, sustained, and expanded through our interactions with other faithing selves in a community of faith. To describe each style of faith is to understand the faith pilgrimage possible for us all. To those styles of faith we turn now.

EXPERIENCED FAITH

No one can determine another's faith and no one can give another faith, but we can be faithful and share our life and our faith with another. Others, regardless of age, can do the same with us, and through this sharing we each sustain, transmit, and expand our faith.

During the preschool and early childhood years, children typically act with "experienced faith." That is to say faith is first experienced enactively. To understand this style of faith we need to remember that children initiate action and respond to our actions. The child explores and tests, imagines and creates, observes and copies, experiences and reacts. Children's actions influence those with whom they interact, and the actions of others influence them. Their acts provide a mirror and a test for those with whom they interact. Not only children live by experienced faith, of course, and while this style of faith represents the earliest style, its characteristics are important and foundational to persons throughout their lives. For example, just as children need to be hugged, caressed, and stroked, so do adults. Regretfully, we seem to have forgotten that and, as a result, adolescent and adult "skin hunger" needs are met by antisocial punching and jabbing. Basic and continuing needs are denied because we have not found socially acceptable ways to affirm hugs between persons of the same and opposite sex. Similarly, throughout our lives, we need to take seriously the needs of experienced faith and, like the child, we need to act in ways that explore and test, observe and copy, imagine and create, experience and react.

Experience is foundational to faith. A person first learns Christ not as a theological affirmation but as an affective experience. For children and adults, it is not so much the words we hear spoken that matter most, but the experiences we have which are connected with those words. Language and experience are interrelated. Experiences of trust, love, and acceptance are important to Christian faith and, regardless of age, the need is always present for experiences consistent with the meanings we attribute to our words. If a person is "used" whenever the word love is spoken, the word love takes on that meaning for the person. A new definition can be learned, but the power of the word will be related to the experiences of the word. That explains why we are called to be doers of the word and not hearers only. As the apostle James writes: " 'Here is one who claims to have faith and another who points to his deeds.' To which I reply: 'Prove to me that this faith you speak of is real though not accompanied by deeds, and by my deeds I will prove to you my faith' " (2:18). We experience and express faith through our interactions with others. The meaning of our vocabulary of faith is directly related to our experience with the words spoken to express that faith.

To be concerned about others' faith is to share our faith with them in word and deed, and to permit them to share their faith with us in similar ways. We can share and respond, but the character of another person's faith cannot be determined. What we can do is provide an environment of sharing and interaction between faithing selves. The responsibility of Christian parents is to endeavor to be Christian with their children, and the responsibility of all Christians is to strive to be Christian with all others.

God makes himself known through his word—his actions. God has not waited to be discovered, but has taken the initiative and addressed his word to humankind through his deeds. In Jesus Christ, the word became flesh. God established the criteria by which we may recognize and understand the word and deed of God in many other and unexpected ways; but for Christian faith, word and deed are never separated.

Experienced faith, therefore, results from our interactions with other faithing selves. And thus the question for a parent to ask is this: What is it to be Christian with my child? To seriously address that question is to discover what sort of environments, experiences, and interactions are necessary for our own and another's life in faith. To live with others in Christian ways, to put our words into deeds and our deeds into words, to share life with another, to be open to influence as well as to influence, and to interact with other faithing selves in a community of Christian faith is to provide the necessary environment for experienced faith.

Will Our Children Have Faith?

If the needs of experienced faith have been adequately met during the childhood and early adolescent years, persons may begin to adopt an affiliative style of faith. During this period persons seek to act with others in an accepting community with a clear sense of identity. All of us need to feel that we *belong* to a self-conscious community and that through our active participation can make a contribution to its life. Persons with affiliative faith need to participate in the community's activities—for example, serving at a fellowship supper, singing in the choir, having a part in the Christmas pageant, participating in a service project, belonging to a group in the church where they know everyone's name and they are missed when absent. Of crucial importance is the sense that we are wanted, needed, accepted, and important to the community. The character of our actions may change with age, but all of us need to feel that we belong to a community and have opportunities to act like someone who truly belongs.

I recall a young man describing his faith pilgrimage and explaining that one of his most significant experiences was in the year that he didn't go to church school but instead read comics, collected the offering, and maintained the attendance records. Why was this experience so important? Because for the first time he felt that he belonged.

A second characteristic of affiliative faith is seen in the dominance of the religious *affections*. Some of us have forgotten or ignored the primal importance of the religion of the heart. We have become too concerned too early with the activities of thinking in Christian education, and we forget that the intuitional mode of consciousness is of equal importance with the intellectual. Indeed, in terms of faith, actions in the realm of the affections are prior to acts of thinking, which is why participation in the arts—drama, music, dance, sculpture, painting, and storytelling—are essential to faith. We need opportunities to act in ways that enhance the religious affections. Opportunities for experiencing awe, wonder, and mystery, as well as chances to sing, dance, paint, and act, are needed by us all. Events like the annual Christmas pageant *are* important. Far greater attention needs to be given to the religion of the heart and those actions that encourage the development of religious affections.

The third characteristic of affiliative faith is a sense of *authority*. What I mean by authority is a community's affirmation of a story and a way of life that judges and inspires its actions. I recall the many times our children told us that everyone else was doing something and we simply replied, "That's fine, but that is not the Westerhoff way." And then we would tell the story of how the Westerhoffs have acted through the years and why that way of life is important to us. Identity and authority go hand-in-hand.

The church must constantly be aware of its story and its way. We need to hear and tell that story, and we need to act so as to internalize it as our story. Child-centered and life-centered education have sometimes forgotten that the story or tradition is of central importance. While faith is first experienced enactively, it is next experienced in images or stories. Learning the community's story is, therefore, an essential for faith.

Throughout our lives, but particularly in the childhood and early adolescent years, we need to belong to and participate in an identity-conscious community of faith. We need to act in ways that nurture our religious affections. And we need to act to internalize, rehearse, and personally own the story which undergirds the community's faith.

SEARCHING FAITH

Providing that the needs of affiliative faith have been met some time during late adolescence, persons may expand into searching faith. Searching faith also has three characteristics. First, there is the action of *doubt* and/or *critical judgment*. Sometimes painful and sometimes celebrative, those with searching faith need to act over against the understanding of faith acquired earlier. We seem to know this, at least in terms of adolescent family behavior, but we have neglected it when considering faith. For example, my teenagers sometimes think I am quite stupid and misguided. And while that is not easy to live with, it is important for them to believe it in order to acquire their own identity. The same is true of faith. In order to move from an understanding of faith that belongs to the community to an understanding of faith that is our own, we need to doubt and question that faith. At this point the "religion of the head" becomes equally important with the "religion of the heart," and acts of the intellect, critical judgment, and inquiry into the meanings and purposes of the story and the ways by which the community of faith lives are essential. Serious study of the story, and engagement with historical, theological, and moral thinking about life become important. The despairs and doubts of the searching soul need to be affirmed and persons need to join others in the intellectual quest for understanding.

A second characteristic of searching faith is *experimentation*. Searching faith requires that we explore alternatives to our earlier understandings and ways, for people need to test their own tradition by learning about others. It is only then that they are able to reach convictions which are truly their own.

And third, searching faith embodies the need to *commit* our lives to persons and causes. Persons with searching faith sometimes appear fickle, giving their lives to one ideology after another, sometimes in rapid succession and on occasion in contradiction. But that is how we learn commitment. How can we know what it means to give our life away until we have learned how to do it? It appears, regretfully, that many adults in the church have never had the benefit of an environment which encouraged searching faith. And so they are often frightened or disturbed by adolescents who are struggling to enlarge their affiliative faith to include searching faith. Some persons are forced out of the church during this state and, sadly, some never return; others remain in searching faith for the rest of their lives. In any case, we must remember that persons with searching faith still need to have all the needs of experienced and dependent faith met, even though they may appear to have cast them aside. And surely they need to be encouraged to remain within the faith community during their intellectual struggle, experimentation, and first endeavors at commitment.

Will Our Children Have Faith?

Providing that the needs of searching faith have been met some time in early adulthood, we may expand into an owned style of faith. This movement from experienced and affiliative faith through searching faith to owned faith is what historically has been called *conversion*. Conversion experiences may be sudden or gradual, dramatic or undramatic, emotional or intellectual, but they always involve a major change in a person's thinking, feeling, and willing—in short, in their total behavior. Due to the serious struggle with doubt that precedes it, owned faith often appears as a great illumination or enlightenment, but in any case it can be witnessed in our actions and new needs. Now people most want to put their faith into personal and social action, and they are willing and able to stand up for what they believe, even against the community of their nurture.

Typically, persons owned by their faith strive to *witness* to that faith in both word and deed. They struggle to eliminate any dissonance between their faith as stated in their beliefs and their actions in the world. The words of St. John: "Whoever claims to be dwelling in Christ, binds himself to live as Christ lived" (I John 2:6), confront them with a new challenge. Persons with owned faith want and need the help and support of others in sustaining and in putting their faith to work. Of course, remember, the characteristics of searching faith are never eliminated, doubt and intellectual struggle continue but are dealt with in new ways. Still liberation, wholeness of life, spiritual health, and identity are known and persons can live a life in but not of the world. The radical demands of the Gospel can now be met.

Owned faith, personal identity, is God's intention for

every person. To reach owned faith (our full potential) is a long pilgrimage in which we need to be provided with an environment and experiences that encourage us to act in ways that assist our expansion of faith. Let us never forget, however, that while the fulfillment of our potential ought to be the aim of all faithing selves, Christ died for us all, and no matter what style of faith we possess none are outside his redeeming grace.

We who are engaged in the church's educational ministry need to commit ourselves to helping each other fulfill our potential as corporate faithing selves, possessed by the Gospel and living according to its radical demands in the world. To do so we need to provide the experiences and environments which encourage those interactions necessary for the expansion of faith. However, it would be well to remember that these styles of faith are not to be used so much to design educational programs for others as to help each of us to understand our personal faith pilgrimage, establish our own needs, and seek interactive experiences with others so we might sustain and expand our own faith. Still, we need to realize that such efforts will contribute to the expansion of others' faith.

CONCLUSIONS

While these four styles of faith, characteristic of the faith pilgrimage of Christians, are important to understand if we are to take seriously enculturation as the means of Christian education, a few comments are in order before I proceed to discuss the implications of this understanding for the educational program of the church.

Will Our Children Have Faith?

First, if we take seriously the styles of faith and faith's expansion, we must conclude that no single educational program for any age-group is valid. Consider adolescents in college (the group I know best). Some enter college ready to act with searching faith and we find them enrolled in college religion courses where the intellectual approach to the Bible and faith meets their needs. The chapel program with its experimental worship services, or even adventures into alternatives such as Zen Buddhist meditation, appeal to them. The college chaplain, who in the name of some ideology calls them to commitment, attracts their devotion and energy. However, there is another group of college students who have never had the needs of affiliative faith satisfactorily met and obviously are not found at the chapel or in religion courses. Instead, they are attracted to various Christian groups which emphasize belonging, the religion of the heart, and the authority of the story. These students will give hours to social service projects and they will talk about their beliefs, but little time is devoted to radical social action. Typically, they consider the religion faculty to be atheists and the chaplain in need of conversion. Conversion, in this case, is understood as the kind of dramatic, sudden, emotional experience many of them experienced as their transition into affiliative faith. We must not depreciate the importance of these students' faith pilgrimage, but rather we should celebrate their expanded faith and support them in their continuing quest.

We also need to be aware that few adults have owned faith, and that is why it is difficult to involve many adults in radical community and social action. Typically, adults have had their faith arrested in the affiliative style. In every church, therefore, a variety of educational environments and experiences that make possible the expansion of faith is needed. Remember, we can never offer a single educational program for all adults or all youth.

A second implication: While we need to provide experiences for each style of faith, we also need to provide experiences that help persons move from one style of faith to another. Such a movement is naturally made possible when life presents us with situations we cannot resolve satisfactorily through actions consistent with our present style of faith, and when we are presented with role models of persons acting more satisfactorily in an expanded style of faith.

Expansion of faith can also be aided or retarded by the community's rites of transition. Typically, for example, we have placed confirmation, which asks for a personal commitment of faith and a commitment to discipleship in the world, at the age when persons need to be encouraged to doubt, question, and experiment. The effect appears to be the arresting of faith. Perhaps confirmation should be moved to early adulthood and a new early adolescent rite celebrated on St. Thomas Day developed. This rite should encourage persons to make a covenant with God and the church and to struggle with their faith as Jacob wrestled with the angels.

If we were to take such insights seriously, we would involve ourselves and others in an educational ministry centered on experiences of interaction between and among persons according to their faith needs. For example, in the preschool and early childhood years we would encourage children to experience the word of God by interacting with those who are striving to be Christian with them through shared experiences. The rite of baptism could initiate persons into this style of faith and prebaptismal preparation for expectant parents could enable them to act in ways helpful to those in experienced faith. First communion during first or second grade could initiate a person into affiliative faith. Intergenerational experiences (in a belonging community where the story is expressed, owned, and known) through participation in the arts could frame the church's educational ministry during the childhood and early adolescent years. The Sunday school (at least as it was understood in the nineteenth century) could provide a structure for such experiences between and among children, youth, and adults of all ages.

At some point in early adolescence we need a ritual to affirm persons in searching faith. As such, this ritual should encourage actions which emphasize the importance of intellectual inquiry and interpretation, bless the existential struggle with doubt, support experimentation with alternative understandings and ways, and facilitate commitment to persons and causes. Spiritual life retreats, short-term interest groups, small intensive study groups, and a variety of interactions in and outside the church between adolescents and adults with owned faith are needed to support searching faith. Confirmation is best saved for early adulthood. Extensive (one or two years) and intensive activities are needed to prepare persons for this important initiation into owned faith. Next comes experiences and interactions based upon action-reflection or the implication of Christian faith for individual and social life. But more of this in the next chapter.

To conclude, when we make enculturation the means of Christian education, we turn to faith. That is, we consider its nature and character and the sorts of experiences and interactions, between and among persons within a community of faith, which encourage and support the expansion of faith. Specific activities and resources may not be easily identified, but at least we can be sure that we are struggling with the right questions. Namely: What is it to be Christian together? How can we live our individual and corporate lives under the judgment and inspiration of the Gospel to the end that God's community is come and God's will is done? What can I bring to share with another as a believer in Christ and a member of his church? What are Christian understandings and ways, and how can we express and experience them with others? How can we be open to one another so that as faithing selves in community we might all expand in our faith?

Answers to such questions will not be simple or easy, but they are at the heart of our educational mission and ministry, and they hold some vital resolutions as to whether or not our children will have faith.

CHAPTER FIVE

Hope for the Future

Christian education is to be thought of, through and
through, as the Christian religion in operation.

George A. Coe

ASSUMING that the community of faith-enculturation paradigm provides us with a frame of reference which
corresponds with our experience and is coherent with our
theological assumptions, we still need to test it for practical
relevance. A good theory is always usable. To be valuable,
the community of faith-enculturation paradigm needs to aid
us in planning and evaluating our church's educational ministry, and I find it does just that. During the last two years I
have worked with a number of different local churches on
various aspects of the paradigm's application. This final
chapter will report a few representative examples.

EVALUATION AND PLANNING

The first use I will share involves educational planning in a
United Church of Christ congregation in the South. To

begin, they defined their educational ministry: "Christian education is all the deliberate, systematic, and sustained efforts we make in any aspect of our parish life which enables us as persons and as a community of faith to be more Christian in our individual and corporate lives." They further defined Christian as "living under the judgment and inspiration of the Gospel to the end that God's will is done and God's community comes." And they agreed that their educational ministry is a lifelong process involving persons of all ages, not confined to the church school but including the total program of their church: (a) their ritual-ceremonial life; (b) the experiences persons have within their congregational life; and (c) their individual and corporate actions in society.

The church's educational ministry, they concluded, is to be judged by how well it (a) sustains and transmits the Christian faith tradition; (b) nurtures the expansion of faith and the spiritual lives of persons; and (c) equips and motivates the church and its members to fulfill their Christian vocation in the world.

Affirming the insights expressed in the last chapter on styles of faith and the expansion of faith through interactions in specific environments, the congregation formulated clearly stated and agreed-upon aims for their church's educational ministry under the headings of *Tradition*, *Persons*, and *Society*. Then, in terms of affiliative, searching, and owned styles of faith, they suggested in general terms what educational experiences needed to be provided. Their conclusions, which follow, are not offered because they are a perfect example to be copied, but because they demonstrate the practical usefulness of the community of faith-enculturation paradigm.

Will Our Children Have Faith?

The Tradition

Aim one: To possess a personal knowledge and understanding of God's revelation as found in the Bible, and to be disposed and able to interpret its meaning for daily individual and social life.

To achieve this aim we need: (a) To be introduced to the biblical story of God's action in history (as found in the stories of the Old and New Testaments) as *our* story; (b) to be involved in an historical, critical interpretation of the biblical story; (c) to be engaged in reflection on current social issues in the light of the biblical story.

Aim Two: To possess a personal knowledge and understanding of the Church's history and be disposed and able to interpret its relevance for daily individual and social life.

To achieve this aim we need: (a) To be introduced to the story of our foreparents' struggles to understand the faith and live faithfully in the world as *our* story; (b) to be involved in a critical historical investigation of the faithfulness of the institutional church throughout its history; (c) to be engaged in reflection on our contemporary striving to be a responsible and responsive community of faith in the light of our history.

Aim three: To possess a personal knowledge and understanding of the Christian faith as expressed historically in the church's creeds, cathechisms, and theological formulations; and be disposed and able to reflect theologically on contemporary life and history.

To achieve this aim we need: (a) To be provided with experiences in community which are consistent with Christian understandings of God, persons, and society; (b) to be introduced to the historic attempts of the people of God to express their faith and to engage in a critical evaluation of our contemporary expressions of faith; (c) to be engaged in reflections on contemporary life in the light of the church's historical affirmations so as to aid us in expressing our faith in meaningful ways today.

Persons

Aim four: To be committed to Jesus Christ as Lord and Savior.

To achieve this aim we need: (a) To be introduced to a community of persons who live their lives as an expression of faith in Jesus Christ as Lord and Savior; (b) to be confronted with a clear intellectual understanding of the Gospel; (c) to be provided with opportunities for a personal decision for or against the affirmation that Jesus Christ is Lord and Savior.

Aim five: To possess a personal relationship with God in Christ and to be aware of God's continual revelation.

To achieve this aim we need: (a) To have our intuitional and historical modes of consciousness enhanced and be introduced to the life of a community of meditation, prayer, and worship; (b) to be aided in our struggles of the soul and be given opportunity to experiment with various forms of meditation, prayer, and worship; (c) to be provided with opportunities to identify God's actions in contemporary history and to celebrate meaningfully in community God's past and present actions in history.

Aim six: To be a faithful and responsible member of the Christian community of faith and to share in its life and mission.

To achieve this aim we need: (a) To be offered experiences which enhance our sense of belonging to a loving, caring, affirming community of faith; (b) to be aided in building a sense of trustful, responsible relationships with others and to be provided opportunities for service in the church's life and mission; (c) to be engaged in meaningful participation in the church's life, worship, fellowship, evangelism, stewardship, service, social action, and governance.

Society

Aim seven: To be aware of our Christian vocation and be able both to make moral decisions in the light of the Christian faith and to be disposed to act faithfully and responsibly in daily individual and corporate life.

To achieve this aim we need: (a) To be provided with experiences foundational to moral decision-making, and be exposed to role models of the Christian life; (b) to be given opportunities to apply Christian faith to individual and social life; (c) to be enabled to act and reflect faithfully and responsibly in our daily individual and corporate lives, to the end that God's kingdom comes and God's will is done.

Aim eight: To understand and be committed to the church's corporate mission in the world for justice, liberation, whole community, peace and the self-development of all peoples, and be disposed and able to engage in the continual reformation of church and society.

To achieve this aim we need: (a) To be introduced to a community of faith engaged in mission and be provided foundations for an awareness of corporate selfhood, justice, freedom, community, and peace; (b) to be given opportunity to commit one's life to social causes for the reformation of church and society; (c) to be equipped and motivated to engage in the reformation of the church and society on behalf of justice, liberation, whole community, peace, and the self-development of all people.

Aim nine: To possess an appreciative understanding of other faith traditions (Christian, Jewish, Muslim, Hindu, etc.) and to be able to enter into meaningful dialogue and action with them without sacrificing the integrity of one's own faith.

To achieve this aim we need: (a) To be exposed to persons of other faith traditions and their customs and ways; (b) to be helped to explore intellectually and experimentally the faith of other persons; (c) to be engaged in meaningful dialogue and actions with persons of other faiths.

HOLISTIC EDUCATION

My second illustration comes from a small United Methodist Church in the Southwest. Working from the community of faith-enculturation paradigm, they examined their situation and proposed a one-year educational program to meet their needs. To accomplish this plan, the ministers and official board of the church went on a retreat where the first step was to write a two-page group description of their church and community:

Our church is situated in a small, expanding community. An increasing number of Roman Catholic Mexican-Americans have moved into the homes which surround our church; and as this has occurred, the congregation has tended to move farther and farther out from the city. As a result, active participation in the church's life and attendance at Sunday services has been negatively affected. Nevertheless, some 300 persons still consider this their church and no other churches exist at present in the emerging suburbs to which they have moved.

Our church is typical of many mainline churches in that it is characterized by its pluralism. There are both the more theologically and socially liberal and the more conservative. There are both the aging and the young, new people and old. Most of the members, however, are upper-middle-class white leaders in the community: bankers, store-keepers, business-owners, ranchers, farm-owners, doctors, lawyers, and teachers. The town's mayor, two members of the town council, three school board members, and the police chief are also church members Our people are most concerned about the Mexican-Americans moving into the community, increasing taxes, and the changing character of this once quiet and secure community.

The church is quite traditional. It has all the committees churches usually have and a large number of organizations: three women's groups, one men's, one couples', two youth's (junior high and senior high). Membership in the youth groups has dwindled off to almost nothing and the parents are concerned. The couples' club is seen as the community's finest "social club," and many belong who do not belong to the church. The women's and men's groups, while primarily social in nature, are still active, live organizations that give significant amounts of time and money to the church.

The church is controlled by the older, long-time residents of the community, and new people have a hard time breaking into its leadership. The pastor emeritus, who had served the church for many years, lives in the community and is loved and respected. He has always had a strong social consciousness but was never able to move the church to action. The district superintendent also attends the church.

Attendance at Sunday services is decreasing. Whereas the older people want a traditional service, the new folk want something different. The church school attendance is also dwindling. Young families frequently go away on weekends, teachers are hard to secure, and children drop out early. No adult Sunday school exists at present.

Recently a crisis has occurred. The fire inspector declared the church school building, which is attached to the church, a fire hazard. A wealthy member is prepared to give a blank check to the church council for the building of a new church school in memory of his wife, who was the Sunday school superintendent for twenty-five years. Some of the members wonder whether anyone will ever use a new church school building, but there are some older members who believe that a new church school building would solve the church's problems.

There are a number of other things about this community that need to be known. A school bond issue for a new school and new educational programs for the increasing number of Mexican-Americans is to be voted on in six months, and feelings are running high on this matter. To complicate matters, Caesar Chavez is said to be coming to organize the farm workers. People are talking about little else.

A number of new, younger families are very much concerned about changing the church's life and being more relevant to community issues. They are getting vocal, but they aren't represented on any official boards or committees.

Will Our Children Have Faith?

Most church members have a feeling something isn't right and they are beginning to hurt. Everyone seems to want some change, but most are looking backward for insight at present. There is a lot of confusion in people's minds about their faith and they are groping. They wish God was more real and life was more meaningful.

By the end of the weekend they had developed a five-part program for educational ministry during the following year. That was three years ago. I will describe each aspect of their proposal and report the results.

Worship

Just prior to this planning meeting the bishops of the United Methodist Church issued a "Call for Peace and Justice Among All Peoples." They decided to make this call and its scriptural foundations the focus of their worship during the Lenten season. Each week a committee of two lay adults, a youth, the pastor, and the pastor emeritus would work together on the sermon. Each sermon (to be limited to ten minutes) was to take the shape of a dialogue between the pastor and the pastor emeritus. Following each dialogue sermon, the congregation was to be given ten minutes to respond. The sermon was to be set in the context of a modified Moravian love feast. That is, coffee and a sweet roll were to be served to each adult and juice and cookies to the children. The children were also given crayons and paper for use during this twenty-minute period. In the context of their sharing in a love feast, the sermon would be preached and responded to. Further the pastor and the pastor emeritus agreed to engage in an increased, systematic program of parish-calling in order to elicit feedback to their sermons. They hoped, through these means, to confront the congregation with the Gospel and its relevance for their social situation.

Church School

Since they did not have a building to meet in, they decided to meet in people's homes one evening each week in intergenerational neighborhood groups. They chose as their content a number of visionary passages from the Scriptures such as: "I will give you rain at the proper time; the land shall yield its produce and the trees of the countryside their fruit. Threshing shall last to vintage and vintage till sowing; you shall eat your fill and live secure in your land" (Lev. 26:4–6). "They shall beat their swords into mattocks and their spears into pruning knives; nation shall not lift up sword against nation nor ever again be trained for war" (Is. 2:4). "They shall know that I am the Lord when I break the bars of their yokes and rescue them from those who have enslaved them. I will give prosperity to their plantations; they shall never again be victims of famine in the land nor any longer bear the taunts of the nations" (Ez. 34:27,29). "The arrogant of heart and mind he has put to rout, he has brought down monarchs from their thrones, but the humble have been lifted high. The hungry he has satisfied with good things, the rich he sent empty away" (Lk. 1:51–53). "Then I saw a new heaven and a new earth, for the first heaven and the first earth had vanished, and there was no longer any sea. I saw the holy city, new Jerusalem, coming down out of heaven from God, made ready like a bride adorned for her husband. I heard a loud voice proclaiming from the throne: 'Now at last God has his dwelling among persons! He will dwell among them and they shall be his people, and God himself will be with them. He will wipe away every tear from their eyes; there shall be an end to death, and to mourning and crying and pain; for the old order has passed away" (Rev. 21:1–4).

Each intergenerational neighborhood group was to explore the meaning of these passages and express them in music, dance, drama, or one of the plastic arts. Then once each month on a Sunday evening they gathered in the fellowship hall of the Roman Catholic Church (across the street from their church) to have supper together and share their creations.

Town Meetings

They decided to hold a series of town meetings to air the issues confronting the community and give the various sides an opportunity to share their views. They proposed that the district superintendent contact the Roman Catholic priests, the Jewish Rabbi, and the ministers of the six other Protestant churches to get their support. Their hope was to hold one town meeting at each church and to place these meetings in the context of worship.

Issue/Action Group

They voted to create a group to explore the school bond issue and engage the congregation in an effort to consider that issue in the light of the Gospel.

Future Planning

The man who offered to give the church a check for a new church school building was asked to chair a planning committee made up of one representative from each board and group in the church and an equal number of youth and adults not in leadership positions. They were to begin with

Bible study on the church and its mission. Following that study, they were to create a five-year vision for their church. From that vision they were to formulate five-year goals. The next step was to consider events which, if they were occurring in two years, would make their five-year goals possible. These events were turned into objectives. Lastly, they were to design strategies and estimate costs for reaching these objectives. They were then to report their plans to the church and seek the support of the congregation.

Persons at the planning retreat were assigned to each of these five task forces and a means was developed to report their plan to the congregation and to secure the congregation's ownership.

When they returned they did just that. The church approved and they proceeded, with some unusual results. Attendance at worship increased. The people found they liked whole families worshiping together, and other changes began to occur in their worship life to make it more meaningful to all ages. The church school was reborn. They decided to continue the intergenerational church school, using the church lectionary as the content for their sessions and the arts as the basis of their activities. All but two Protestant churches cooperated in the town meetings. A new ecumenical spirit emerged, and while there was still much disagreement over community issues, they saved the community from being blown apart. Due in part to the "religious educational" efforts of the issue-action group, the bond issue passed.

The planning group proposed for the future: (a) family worship; (b) the renovation of the church (rather than the building of a new building); (c) the creation of an endowment for church mission and program; and (d) the continuation of an intergenerational church school. The renovation plans were quite radical. They voted to take the pews out of the church and turn the nave into an all-purpose room for education, worship, and fellowship, with rugs on the floor and an adjoining kitchen and library meeting room. The basement was turned into a day care center for the community, church offices, and storage. The intergenerational church school was moved from homes to the church and was held on Sunday evenings in the context of celebration, learning, and fellowship. Worship for all ages continued in the morning. The day care center became an ecumenical venture open to the community. The church raised funds for the renovation and the chairperson of the planning group created an endowment to support the day care center and other church programs.

In the process they lost fifty-two members (many of them the older, more affluent members). They also gained twenty-eight new members (a net loss of twenty-four), but they increased pledges so that the church was more financially secure than before. More important, the church had come to life.

A NEW CHURCH SCHOOL FOR DEPENDENT FAITH

The descriptions that follow are of a variety of educational programs that are consistent with the community of faith-enculturation paradigm. Each is an example of a reformed church school. They may or may not meet on Sundays, and they may or may not meet every week. When they do meet, they bring together children, youth, and adults for common activities. Music, dance, drama, the plastic arts, and film-making provide the dominant forms of expression. Integral to their life is celebration; the focus of program is the Christian story, and the primary concern is for opportunities to be Christian together.

The following examples are based upon actual churches, all under 300 members, of several denominations, and without employed professional educators. The first is a small New England congregation. At a church meeting each year the people decide on a series of themes for their Sunday school. Last year they chose Moses and the Exodus, Advent-Christmas, Contemporary Christians, and Life in the Early Church. The Sunday school meets intergenerationally for four blocks of time during the year, and each thematic unit is assigned to a group of families who create and lead the Sunday school for that period. The first block of time runs from the first day of school through Thanksgiving. During the summer those who are interested prepared a dramatization of episodes in Moses' life. In the first week they presented a dramatization; the next week interest groups were formed.

There was an opportunity to make unleavened bread, and to create poetry of modern parallels to Moses' experience—and an art group illustrated the poetry. Other activities were taken from *The Jewish Catalogue*, one of the truly great resources needed for the Sunday school of the future. There was even a group who used the dark, dirt-filled, junk-strewn basement of the church to create a simulation of the Israelites' faith during the darkness of the long exodus. Two weeks of these activities led to two weeks of planning for a Seder, using Waskow's *Freedom Seder* as the basis for their celebration. Then came two weeks of preparation for a special Thanksgiving celebration, where there was an opportunity to identify the Congregational Puritan history with the Exodus. The unit ended with a grand Thanksgiving celebration, at which five grains of corn were put at everyone's place, a child asked why, and the story was told of the year when that was all their foreparents had for which to give thanks. After a few weeks people were ready to begin the Advent-Christmas theme.

Another example is a midwestern Sunday school that used the church lectionary to determine their Sunday school program, in which the Scripture lesson read in church each week would be used as the text for the sermon and the focus of the Sunday school hour. The week I observed, the lesson was Romans 5:20: "Moreover the law entered, that the offense might abound. But where sin abounded, grace did much more abound." The theme was "You are Accepted." In this church, people twelve years and older volunteer to be responsible for organizing diverse activities around the theme. They gather during the previous week for planning.

On this particular week, after they sang some hymns and folk songs, the lesson for the day was read and various activities were announced. One teen-age girl said that she wanted to talk about acceptance and paint pictures, and a group of ten gathered around a table she had set up in the hall. They talked about those in the community who were not accepted, and she commented that the Christian church accepts everyone, even if they don't deserve it. Then she suggested they all paint pictures. Most drew Indians, representing those not accepted, but one boy drew a tremendous monster urinating. The girl, in a validating manner, praised all the pictures and put them up on the wall. I watched the boy's face and saw it light up. I suspect that he had set out to test her statement that the Christian church accepts everyone, and as a result of her marvelously gracious act he had experienced grace.

In the same church that week, another scene was taking place in which one little boy spent the entire time destroying other people's work. No one felt that the situation was handled very well. During the break between Sunday school and family worship, the leaders for the week gathered to reflect on their experiences while the rest of the congregation engaged in fellowship and recreation. On this day the boy was the focus of concern. One of the adults asked if anyone knew what might be the matter. "Sure," said a teen-ager. "He wants attention." Well, what were they going to do about that? "Let's divide him up," one junior high girl suggested. "That is," she explained, "let's each take him for a week and be his special friend and give him all the attention he needs." They did, and that young boy also experienced grace. It would not be too dramatic to say that some day, when recalling his memories of the Sunday school, he will tell about this experience.

Another example is a West Coast church whose Christian education committee decided that it wanted to give a rebirth to the Sunday school. They were tired of cajoling people to teach and they were disturbed that children had stopped coming, so they scrapped the curriculum and decided to focus on drama, art, and music. Someone remembered reading about the old medieval plays that used to enact principal episodes from the Old and New Testaments. In medieval times the plays were undertaken by the craft guilds, analogous to our present-day trade unions, and when possible, the guilds presented plays that dealt with themes associated with their craft: the bakers presented the Last Supper, the goldsmiths the Adoration of the Magi, the shipwrights the Noah play, and so on. All the actors were amateurs, and scripts were usually superfluous because most of the players were illiterate. This church had families sign up in groups according to their favorite pastimes. There were such groups as mountain climbers, sailors, gourmet cooks, and musicians. Each group was given a biblical episode and told to create two dramas, one of the biblical story and one a contemporary expression of the story. Planning the drama was to be half the fun, and everyone was to have a part. There were costumes and props to be made and parts to be learned. Then during Lent everyone gathered and each group presented its play and involved everyone in it. This was followed by discussion and refreshments. The plays went so well that they decided to do it again the following year.

Another Southern church I'd like to mention chose the church year as its organizing principle. Activities were to be created which would help the congregation prepare for each season of the church year, and a season was assigned to existing groups and organizations in the church. The youth group was responsible for Pentecost, so they created an interesting group of activities for the weeks before Pentecost, and every child, youth, and adult chose a group to participate in. One group planned to bake and decorate a mammoth birthday cake for the church; another made banners for a parade symbolizing the works of the Holy Spirit; another made ceramic medallions to be given to those persons who renewed their confirmation vows at the Pentecost celebration. Other groups worked on original vocal and instrumental music, on a dramatic production of the account of Pentecost in Acts, and a last group designed and planned games from around the world for the church's birthday party. On Pentecost they united their labors for a fantastic celebration.

RELIGION OF THE HEAD FOR SEARCHING FAITH

One day a minister posted a large advertisement on the church bulletin board. It read: "Wanted—Film-Makers." "Subject: This Church *vs.* The Gospel." A group of eight persons gathered at the appointed time and spent their first two meetings viewing short films, experimenting with a Super-8 projector, a previewer, an editing machine, and discussing the hows of film-making. They decided their first task was to understand the Gospel, since that was integral to the concept of the film. Ten weeks were spent in concentrated study of the synoptic Gospels, using the tools of biblical scholarship. At the same time they shot as much footage of church life as they could afford, and at the end of the eight weeks they began the process of putting together their film. Another six weeks and they had a film and tape entitled "The Judgment," which was then shown at a church supper and followed by a discussion. As a result, a new four-week seminar on the synoptic Gospels was led by the film-makers.

Another group used the *Learning To Be Free* resource, which I developed with Joe Williamson and a group of young people from a Congregational Church in Massachusetts (part of the United Church of Christ's Shalom

Will Our Children Have Faith?

Curriculum). In this resource is a paperback, *Liberation Letters*, that contains a series of five letters I had written to youth from various places around the world. This church sent a copy of *Liberation Letters* to each eleventh- and twelfth-grader, including those who hadn't been seen in some time. In the book was a postcard to be returned to the church if they were interested in joining a group to work on liberation from a Christian perspective. Those who returned the card were notified of a place and time to meet, and copies of a process workbook, developed and tested by the youth in Massachusetts, were made available.

The process developed like this: They worked at building a learning, witnessing, faith community, and they explored the Christian understanding of liberation. Then they identified where they experienced oppression. (In their case they concluded that they were oppressed by their public school library because it contained only books from a single perspective; that is, there was no Malcolm X and no Karl Marx.) They developed a strategy in which they asked the church for funds for books. No one asked what books, but they were given a hundred dollars with which they bought the books they felt were missing and presented them to the school librarian. Troubled by the titles, she turned them over to the principal, who passed them on to the superintendent. Soon the school board had a decision to make and the whole community was involved. When word got back to the church there were a number of upset adults. As part of their strategy the youth had anticipated trouble and had planned a series of meetings to aid the church in looking at this issue in the light of the Scriptures, the church's history, and its theological affirmations. After six weeks of struggling with the issue, the public school decided to accept approximately one-third of the books, and the church voted to put the others in its library.

Another example is found in a church that decided to build serious study into all its boards and committee meetings as well as other church gatherings. One evening the youth and adult choirs had gathered to plan a "hymn sing" for Lent. They began by making large name tags which also included each person's belief about the relationship between Jesus and God. Next they went around the room looking for those with whom they agreed. After forming groups, each group was to find a hymn which expressed their beliefs and write it on newsprint.

Following this exercise they saw the United Church of Christ filmstrip, "The Council of Nicaea," and then discussed the Nicene creed and summarized its contents: Christ is God; Christ is man; Christ is one. Then they reviewed the beliefs expressed in their hymns to make sure that each of these theological statements was present and a balanced orthodox understanding of Jesus Christ was affirmed. Putting the hymns in the order to be sung, they also wrote up short histories of each hymn and a summary statement of its theological affirmation. Not only had they created an exciting hymn sing in the three hours, but they had learned much about Christian theology.

One last example is based upon a series of two-day spiritual life retreats that brought together a number of events and made possible an unusually "concentrated" educational experience. There were experiments in worship following the monastic hours, silence and meditation, critical Bible study, sharing of theological doubts and questions, exploration of other religions and their cultic life, discussions on commitment and the Christian life and fellowship. Persons committed themselves to three of these retreats during the year, and after the third one they were responsible for sharing their struggles of the soul, intellectual quests, insights, and resolutions with the congregation.

Through these concentrated educational experiences in which some of the needs of searching faith—intellectual inquiry, action, and experimentation in community—are met, persons can be nurtured in the expansion of their faith.

WITNESS-ACTION EDUCATION FOR OWNED FAITH

One of the problems inherent in learning to apply our faith to life situations is the context in which we do our learning. You can teach a course in business ethics, but that does not mean people can or will use their learning when confronted by ethical issues in their office. People best learn to apply faith to life when they learn to do it in the context of their decision-making, a fact that I discovered in a fascinating way.

One day I was about to enter the hospital room of a parishioner and I met her doctor, another parishioner. He exclaimed, "My medical oath doesn't make sense anymore. I have kept Mrs. X alive in a vegetable state at a cost no one can afford for six months, and I can continue to do so. The question now is: Ought I continue? And no one is helping me to solve that question." With that, he ran off and I went in to see Mrs. X. That night I went to see him and asked if other doctors were asking such questions, and if they ever discussed them. The result was a weekly two-hour luncheon, at a reserved table in the doctors' dining room of the hospital, in which we began each session with a case study of a patient that presented a moral dilemma. Then we sought to find solutions that were consistent with Christian faith.

From this experience I developed a number of principles for adult religious education: (1) Go where they are. Don't bring them to the church but engage in education in the midst of where they make their decisions and act. (2) Have a homogeneous group, not everyone alike, but people with the same questions, problems, and needs. (3) Never ask for more than five weeks' commitment. (4) Begin where they are, with their problems. (5) Work toward some action.

Through the years, these principles have proven particularly valuable for persons who are struggling to put their faith into action in the world. I have had experiences with groups of educators, lawyers, doctors, and government officials. One group which worked particularly well involved New York business people who had an hour-and-twenty-minute commute on a train each morning and night. In twenty minutes they read the *New York Times* and the *Wall Street Journal* and then they slept. So we rented one of the railroad cars. They all read their papers and then we had an hour to discuss business case studies. When we got to New York, I could experience their life, see them in action, and develop new cases to be addressed.

CONCLUSIONS

Examples could go on and on. Over the past two years I have found the community of faith-enculturation paradigm relevant, in practice, and indeed valuable as a theoretical frame of reference for reforming the church's educational ministry. Of course, a great deal more work needs to be done on the paradigm itself, as well as on its application. In this short tract I have only sought to introduce some pre-liminary conclusions that have been developing for a few years, but that needed to be expressed. Now the critical help of all those people in local churches who share my concern for the church's educational mission and ministry is needed. Together, revisions, clarifications, and expansions can be made. I suspect that we will make some mistakes, but future generations, aware of our shortcomings, surely will reform religious education once again. I hope to live long enough to support those reforms, for I have no desire to hold on to the present as the final word. Rather, my only wish is to be faithful to the Gospel and the needs of our day. That, I have striven to do. While time will reveal how successful I have been, I do believe that the community of faith-enculturation paradigm provides, for today, a frame of reference and an understanding of religious education that adequately and imaginatively addresses the question: Will our children have faith? Further, I believe it suggests ways to engage in religious education that can insure a posi-tive response to that question. Our children will have faith if we have faith and are faithful. Both we and our children will have Christian faith if we join with others in a worship-ing, learning, witnessing Christian community of faith. To evolve this sort of community where persons strive to be Christian together is the challenge of Christian education in the years ahead.